Dare To Be Extraordinary

A Collection of Positive Life Lessons from African American Fathers

Dare To Be Extraordinary

A Collection of Positive Life Lessons from African American Fathers

Leslie M. Gordon & William K. Middlebrooks

ISBN 978-1-300-74100-8

Table of Contents

Acknowledgements

"Son, the only difference between living an ordinary life and an extraordinary life is your willingness to do the *extra* in everything you undertake."

−Arthur Middlebrooks (1916-1998)

To my sons Arthur and Andrew,

What a blessing it is to be your father!

My greatest accomplishment and joy in life has been raising you to become men of substance, character, integrity, and compassion. I've marveled at the growth, maturity, deep thinking, and success that each of you has demonstrated throughout your lives. I'm proud of you both. Not only for the men you have become but more importantly, for the countless contributions you have already made and will continue to make to our community and our country. I know that in many forms and fashions that I have dared each of you to become extraordinary, and it has been my privilege and honor to share with you the many positive life lessons that both your grandfathers, Arthur "Chick" Middlebrooks and James Rose, Sr. shared with me. As always, be proud of what you have accomplished, but never be satisfied!

Love, Dad

To my wife Karla,

I am because we are, and for the past thirty years you have absolutely been the wind beneath my wings.

Your loving husband, Bill

To my mother and father, Alice Middlebrooks and Arthur "Chick" Middlebrooks,

Thank you for all the years of unconditional love, support, and guidance. I can say without hesitation, I never went a day in my life where I felt unloved or unsupported even when I tested your patience and nerves. I was so blessed to have you as parents and not a day goes by since each of you has passed that I don't reflect on a positive life lesson you shared with me. I give special thanks for being able to call you mom and dad. I've tried to live my life as you raised me to do and pass along the enormous wealth of love, wisdom, and support to Arthur and Andrew that you both so unselfishly gave me.

I hope I've made you proud, and God bless your souls.

Your loving son, Bill

To Leslie Gordon, my co-author,

My special thanks and appreciation for your commitment, passion, and contributions to this project.

Bill

To the extraordinary men and women featured in this book,

What a great living inspiration and wonderful life legacy each of you have created that serves to honor the role, influence, and commitment your father shared with you. I greatly appreciate your support for this project by way of the trust and confidence you have placed in Leslie and me to showcase your fathers' lives as well as your own extraordinary lives. More importantly, I thank you for sharing your very personal stories that gives the reader great insight into and a resounding confirmation that wonderful, caring, and engaged African American fathers really do exist. Clearly your fathers have made a real difference in your lives, and I'm confident wherever he is today, he looks with great pride on all of your accomplishments.

Bill

Acknowledgements

Writing about each of these exceptional men and women and telling the rich stories of how their fathers shaped their lives has been an indescribable journey for me. I extend my deepest thanks to Bill Middlebrooks for trusting me with such a meaningful project.

In talking with, researching, and thinking about each son and daughter featured here, I developed a deeper level of respect for all fathers who make their presence felt, not just for a day or a year, but for a lifetime. In having the great privilege to peer into and write about the lives of these extraordinary CEOs, cultural icons, athletes, politicians, business leaders, activists, doctors, newsmakers, and some of the best and brightest minds of our time, I laughed and I cried, I screamed and on some days I threw my hands up in frustration. But most of all, my heart was full—from the very first chapter to the very last. I came to genuinely understand and appreciate the power, strength, and courage of our beloved fathers.

Each day I am reminded of my own extraordinary fathers. That's fathers with an 's' because my biological father is not the only man who shaped my life. Without guidance from other special father figures who provided love, laughter, support, and a swift kick when I needed it, I would have never been able to put pen to paper and work with Bill to create this wonderful tribute to African American fathers.

To my father, Leslie, I say, thank you. It's been thirty-one long years since I've seen your face, heard your laugh, and stood quietly with my eyes lowered to the ground as you scolded me for having a crush on a middle school boy. Yet, I still miss you as if it were just yesterday that you slipped away. From you I learned to be smart, bold, and confident. I learned that I didn't have to play the hand that was dealt. Instead, I could create my own hand. From you, I learned drive, determination and that nothing or no one could stop me. No amount of time will diminish my love for you. Every time I look in the mirror, I see your face and I am reminded of the love we shared. I miss you, Dad.

To my grandfather, Romuald, I say, thank you. You were not only my grandfather, you were my heart, and I loved you fiercely. You were always, always there for me—bandaging my knees when I skinned them, teaching me how to drive, picking me up from college during my breaks, sitting proudly in the University of Chicago's Rockefeller Chapel when I received my Master's degree, going on walks with me, fixing things in my home, and just loving me. Grandad, you were the rock of our family and a beautiful example of a kind-hearted gentleman who always put family first. Although you've been gone for almost five years, I still reflect on how tremendously blessed I am to have been surrounded by your love.

To my stepfather, Bahati, I say, *mahalo nui loa*. You taught me that love and life do not always have to come in a neat little traditional package. You taught me what living life on one's own terms looks like. You gave me a sense of freedom and a connection with life and God's earth that I would never have found otherwise. *Aloha wau ia 'oe.*

To my Uncle Harrison, I say thank you. Thank you for always treating me like a special niece and showing me what a cool, present father should be, which included listening to The Spinners and The O'Jays, and playing golf! When my dad passed away, I looked to you as a surrogate father, and you never let me down. The love you've shown and the lessons you've shared will stay with me always.

To George, I say thank you. You loved my mother like no one else and taught us all so much about character and strength, kindness, and compassion. Your spirit will live forever in my heart.

To Team Leslie, you provided the kind of support I could have only imagined. I thank you for listening to me, teaching me, asking thought-provoking questions, and providing helpful critiques. Thank you especially to my amazing sons, Stephen Paul and Landon, who have an extraordinary father and father figures in their lives—for which I am eternally grateful. I love you both with my whole heart and I am so pleased to see how you're growing into loving, responsible, strong-willed men. Throughout this process, you encouraged me from start to finish and kept me on task. Mom "just kept swimming," and now look what we've accomplished!

To my favorite daughter, Taylor, for years I knew that I would have three children and you, my dear, suddenly walked into my life with your radiant smile and your beautiful heart. You are a bright light in my life, and I adore you.

To my mother, Paulette, Aunt Carole (my other mother), my sisters, Zurii and Stephanie, and my dear friend Ayala. You each inspire me every day. I love you and appreciate the closeness we share more than you'll ever know. You know how instrumental you've been as I breathed life into this project. Thank you.

To my brothers Paul and Todd, you have both become extraordinary husbands and fathers. I love you both, and from you I learn something new about committed, fun, remarkable fathers all the time.

To Jill and Felicia, without your help I can assure you I would have been lost. Thank you.

Finally, to my husband, Ed, I don't even think the words thank you are powerful enough to express how I feel. I thank God for you every day, truly I do. Thank you for loving me and being patient. Thank you for listening and talking with me even when you had your own work to do. Thank you most of all for showing in word and in deed what true fatherhood and manhood are all about. Your life and the examples of gravitas, integrity, and honor that you set continue to amaze me. I could not have chosen a better partner to share my life with. I appreciate all that you are and all that we have yet to become—together.

Leslie

Preface

My purpose for doing this book is two-fold. First, I want to bring greater focus and recognition to men who everyday readily accept the role and challenges of fatherhood. The old adage of "we reap what we sow" applies to good fathers as well, and I want to be part of a positive conversation that highlights and sows the seeds for great fathers. To that end, it is important to provide real life examples and celebrate men being engaged fathers as a way of offering men a roadmap in the raising of their own children. Second, I want the positive stories and messages featured in this book to both encourage and inspire fathers, particularly African American men, to step forward and embrace the responsibility, the joys, and the challenges that being an engaged father can provide.

Our mothers have played this role for a very long time and our current status in society tells us that while the role of mothers is important, the role of fathers is vital to increasing the odds and opportunities for our children's success. Society is replete with example after example of the negative impact of not having a father present in the lives of their children. (i.e. children without a father present in the home are eight times more likely to be victims of maltreatment by a live-in partner.[1]) We cannot and will not maintain our position in the world as the greatest nation on the earth if more fathers don't step up to do what is right by their children and dare to raise them to lead extraordinary lives.

This book is not meant to dwell on the negative things we know happen when a father is not present, but rather to focus and celebrate the many positive things that will happen when we are present in the lives of our children. Our society seems to focus more on the negative than the positive image of fatherhood. Rather than be another accomplice to that form of thinking, I decided as an engaged father that I wanted to be a part of something more positive, something bigger. I want to shine a bright light on the wonderful things that being a father can bring a man while also letting him know that while we don't get an instruction manual with the birth of our children there are many examples of African American men who, regardless of their level of education and/or material wealth, accepted the challenge to raise their children and in many cases put them on a path to lead extraordinary lives.

There is no doubt that the men and women whose respective stories are featured in this book have all lead extraordinary lives, by any measure, and have made many contributions to our society. I want the reader to know that I deliberately chose to feature people that are both famous and not so famous because I want to present a diverse and wide range of positive examples. While it's always fun

---

[1] The 6th Edition of Father Facts – National Fatherhood Initiative

and interesting to learn about famous people it's equally important to know and celebrate the numerous examples in our community, of people doing great and wonderful things with their lives. On a daily basis, these men and women live quiet lives, yet provide loud and compelling testimonies for their fathers' positive impact.

I hope the reader recognizes and appreciates the range of experiences that are showcased in the stories. For me, I come away from my conversations with these extraordinary men and women with a clear understanding that while they each enjoyed a unique type of relationship their fathers, they all shared a common theme or lesson that each father imbedded within them: No matter where you go and what you do in your life you should approach everything with a sense of *PRIDE*.

My interpretation of the lessons for this sense of *PRIDE* focuses on taking <u>P</u>ersonal <u>R</u>esponsibility <u>I</u>n <u>D</u>elivering <u>E</u>xcellence by always being prepared, professional and performance oriented; being responsive, resourceful and respectful; being innovative, involved and taking the initiative; being demanding of oneself, determined and dedicated; being enthusiastic, excellent and executing with precision in all that you do.

Finally, when I set out to write this book with Leslie, I thought long and hard about what would be the promise and guiding principles for the book. I wanted to make sure that in writing the stories, we would work very hard to accomplish the following:

- *Recognize and uplift* the role of African American men as engaged and loving fathers.

- *Educate and reinforce* within the African American community and beyond, that African American men have been and continue to be excellent fathers.

- *Offer a roadmap* of ideas for African American fathers on how to raise extraordinary sons and daughters.

- *Inspire* African American men to take a leadership role in raising their sons and daughters.

- *Entertain* with personal and revealing stories about how some men and women were positively influenced by their fathers to live full and meaningful lives.

- Begin a *new, positive conversation* about African American men and their role and influence in raising their sons and daughters.

I hope we have succeeded in keeping to this promise.

William "Bill" K. Middlebrooks

Hear, my child, and accept my words, that the years of your life may be many. I have taught you the way of wisdom; I have led you in the paths of uprightness. When you walk, your step will not be hampered; and if you run, you will not stumble. Keep hold of instruction; do not let go; guard her, for she is your life.

–Proverbs 4:10-13

Robin Roberts

National Broadcast Journalist

"My father was a true officer and a gentleman. There was nothing grandiose about Colonel Lawrence E. Roberts. He was just a good, good, good man."

Robin Roberts brings joy, honesty, and news to millions of loyal Good Morning America viewers each day. When she laughs, we laugh. When she cries, we cry. Roberts has an uncanny way of making us feel her joy *and* her pain, and her extraordinary brand of journalism can't be taught in school or learned in a newsroom. Off camera, she is just as humble and authentic as she is on camera. People are naturally drawn to her just as they were drawn to her loving father, Colonel Lawrence Edward Roberts, a man she describes as a true officer and a gentleman.

Although the Emmy Award-winning broadcast journalist spent most of her career covering the competitive world of sports, she is just as adept at reporting the unimaginable devastation of Hurricane Katrina or engaging viewers in her lighter on-camera moments as she dines at the White House with the Queen of England. After working as a sports anchor and reporter in several

Southern markets from 1983 to 1990, Roberts got her big break on ESPN's Sports Center as the first African American female anchor, a position she held from 1990 to 2005. She became a featured reporter for Good Morning America in 1995 and continued to work for both ESPN and ABC for years before being promoted to co-anchor of Good Morning America in 2005. With co-anchor, George Stephanopoulos, Roberts led the broadcast back to the top of the ratings in April 2012, making it the number one morning show for the first time in sixteen years.

Roberts was a top athlete in college, setting records as a women's basketball player at Southeastern Louisiana University where her jersey now hangs from the rafters. In 2012, she was inducted into the Women's Basketball Hall of Fame for her contributions to and impact on women's basketball both on and off the court. Roberts has had an illustrious career that just keeps getting better and better, according to millions of resolute fans who have fallen in love with her unique insight, her intellect, and her 1,000-watt smile.

Roberts was born in Tuskegee, Alabama on November 23, 1960 to Lawrence and Lucimarian Roberts. Her father, Colonel Roberts, was born in New Jersey in 1922. He was immensely proud of his father's family, who owned a New Jersey-based taxi service at a time when it was almost unheard of for an African American family to own a business. Right after the Great Depression, Colonel Roberts's father owned his own home at a very young age when most black families rented and couldn't afford to buy a home. Growing up, Colonel Roberts was interested in two things: dentistry and aviation. He viewed dentistry as an honorable profession because a successful dentist owned a practice in his neighborhood and as a child he observed that the dentist made a good living. At a young age, Colonel Roberts thought he would go to dental school and become a dentist, but his true passion was for aviation. The future pilot would go down to the basement of his childhood home with a sawed off broomstick handle and pretend the handle was the joystick of an airplane. People would say to him, "What are you doing? You'll never fly. We can't even ride the bus, and you're talking about flying a plane one day?" Colonel Roberts refused to listen to the naysayers. He knew that one day he would fly.

Colonel Roberts met the lovely Lucimarian, originally from Akron, Ohio, on the campus of Howard University in Washington, DC in 1942. Both Lawrence and Lucimarian came from humble beginnings and were the first in their families to go to college. Through the years, Lucimarian loved to tell the story of how much of a gentleman Lawrence was. She would see him on Howard's campus walking to the cafeteria and as Roberts describes it, her mother would conveniently run into him on "accident slash purpose." "My dad was such a gentleman and would pay for her meals," Robin says. Lucimarian also expressed how excited she was to see the distinguished college co-ed coming to her dormitory. This was, of course, in the 1940s when the Howard University women's dormitory had a dorm mother, and the gentleman caller had to ring a doorbell to summon the young lady he came to call on. Lucimarian waited patiently for her bell to ring, only to find out that Colonel Roberts had come to take one of her sorority sisters on a date. She was crushed, and it didn't work out between them at the time. But, they developed a friendship that eventually turned into true love.

Colonel Roberts enlisted in the United States Air Force, and the young couple married in 1947. Before Lucimarian knew it, they were living in Japan, and the oldest of their four children was born a year later. As a military family, they moved a total of twenty-seven times, and all four of the Roberts children were born in different states depending on where Colonel Roberts was stationed at the time.

As a proud American and a member of the Armed Forces, it really hurt Colonel Roberts to be discriminated against because of the color of his skin. During one of many moves before Roberts, the youngest, was born, the family showed up at their new military base only to be turned away. One white guard said to Colonel Roberts, "Boy, you're going to have to find somewhere else to stay tonight. Come back in the morning and maybe somebody else will let you on base, but not on my watch." "My dad could take a lot, but anytime he felt that you were disrespecting him or more important, his family, that really hurt him," Robin says. Colonel Roberts never had to raise his voice when dealing with these situations that would either break or anger the average man.

In New Jersey in the early 60s, Roberts's brother, Butch, was hauled into jail by the military police for being in the wrong place at the wrong time. Butch kept telling the military police, "My father is an officer! My father is an officer!" And yet they insisted he was a liar. Lawrence went to get his son from jail. Lucimarian was livid. Roberts had never heard her mom swear before that night. Lucimarian told her husband, "You tell these S.O.B.'s exactly who you are! You need to get angry and pitch a fit!" Lawrence refused to take that kind of stance. He cleared up the matter and brought his son home without raising his voice because he always felt there was a better way of going about solving such matters. Colonel Roberts had the unique ability to be a peacemaker without letting people run over him, and he passed down these important life lessons of strength and humility to each his four children. He was a problem solver. He felt that the universe was on the side of justice and that he would prevail without bending, breaking, or resorting to violence. "My dad never cowered," Robin says. "He had a quiet strength, and he believed in what he believed in. He was able to get his point across in a very dignified and passionate, but quiet way."

In Roberts's eyes, her father was a gentle giant. He was compassionate and although he had a straight-laced, buttoned up persona, and a deep voice, there was a real softness to him. She recalls that her mother would try to discipline her and her siblings, but when their father would walk through the door all he had to do was clear his throat and the kids would scatter. Colonel Roberts was always big about going to church together as a family on Sundays. If the Roberts kids didn't go to church, they couldn't play. That was one of his rules. When Roberts was four years old, the family attended a church retreat at Lake George in the Adirondack Mountains of upstate New York. Her parents explicitly told her not to go out to the lake by herself, but she didn't listen. It was the last day of the church retreat. Colonel and Mrs. Roberts could not find her and quickly went into full panic mode searching frantically for little Robin. Finally, they spotted her sitting at the end of the pier, dangling her feet over the water, swinging her tiny legs back and forth like a pendulum. Her father quietly came up behind her because he didn't want to startle her and cause her fall into the water. He came up very gently and scooped her up into his warm embrace. This is when they knew she was safe. Roberts thinks that's what she always subconsciously felt—a warm embrace from her first love, her dad.

Roberts recalls her father telling silly daddy jokes—the ones that only she and her brother, Butch, got. Her dad had a wonderful, hearty laugh and could barely get his jokes out before doubling over with laughter. Robin, her mother and sisters would look at him and one of the girls would shout, "Daddy, that really wasn't funny, but you already know that." She recalls one year the family bought the Colonel blue jeans as a gift. "Bless his heart, he did wear them, but he looked so uncomfortable," she shares, laughing. "We were like, 'Daddy, you don't have to wear them but he wore them anyway. If he could have slept in a suit and tie, I think he would have.'"

Although many assume Roberts learned sports from her father, the truth is that she got much of her sports knowledge from her mom. Her dad, however, loved sports, especially baseball and even bowling. She has fond memories of taking up bowling when she was about eight years old. The young bowler got her own bowling ball and recalled that her dad didn't have the most masculine form when he bowled. This was particularly funny to Roberts because her dad was such a "man's man." He would do a little dance before he rolled the ball, which made Roberts laugh out loud. She appreciated that her dad, though an incredibly busy military officer, took the time to bowl with her and she cherishes all of their moments together.

In 1969, he was promoted to Colonel, a rank held by only thirty-five black men in the United States at the time. Roberts loved to answer the telephone: "Colonel Roberts' quarters, Robin speaking." Her father would just look at her as if to say, "Oh my gosh, what have I raised?" Roberts loved the structure of having a military father. When the future broadcaster was ten years old, her family lived on Keesler Air Force base in Biloxi, Mississippi where her father was a commander. Her uncle and his family came to visit. Excited, Roberts wanted to run outside to greet them the moment she saw her uncle's car pull up in the yard. Her dad calmly put his arm around her shoulders and said, "No." He wanted her to conduct herself like a young lady and expressed that when they got in the house, she could jump up and down and knock her cousins over like a Labrador retriever if she chose to.

Roberts got the lesson her dad was teaching her that day. She respected her father's position and never felt that he stifled her. She understood that as an officer, he was very aware of the spotlight and the attention they received as a black family in Mississippi. And yet, he stayed true to himself. He was a proud black man and proud of his family.

Colonel Roberts never had to sit Roberts or any of his children down to talk about going to college or doing something important with their lives. Greatness was just expected. Roberts spent her childhood watching her parent's example. She remembers a time in college when she had her heart set on buying a motorcycle, and she felt that she needed to tell somebody. So she called her sister, Dorothy, and said, "I saved up my money, and I'm buying a motorcycle. But don't tell mom and dad!"

Her sister replied, "Oh Robin, why are you doing this to me?"

About an hour later her telephone rang, and Roberts's roommate announced that her mom was calling. She picked up the phone to talk to her mother. "Dorothy won't tell us what it is but she said that you're going to do something you shouldn't do, so technically she didn't violate your trust," her mother said.

Roberts told her mother the truth: "I'm getting a motorcycle tomorrow."

Immediately her mother put her dad on the phone. Her father firmly said to his youngest child, "Under no circumstances will you buy a motorcycle. No daughter of mine will do that. You know it's a deathtrap. You have a car to get you from point A to point B.

You know, if that's gonna be the case you can bring that car home, and you can just ride your bicycle to your classes." Her father went on and on until Roberts relented. "Fine, I won't buy a motorcycle!" Robin said and hung up.

Many years later, her dad asked her, "Did I handle that right, Robin? Because I really don't think I handled that right with you."

Robin replied, "Dad I'm fine! It's okay. I've really let it go." This lesson and his firm but gentle guidance has always stayed with her.

Roberts's father influenced her career choice because it was an adventure being the daughter of Colonel Lawrence E. Roberts. She wanted to see even more of the world because her dad had already shown it to her and because she had already gotten a taste of it, she knew that as an adult a nine to five job wasn't for her. Roberts felt she needed a career that would feed her appetite for adventure. She wanted a career that would allow her to travel and meet different people. She wasn't afraid to make friends or move somewhere and not know anyone.

"My father loved, loved, loved flying until the day he died," Robin says. "He had little private planes that he got with a bunch of his buddies. I don't know how those things stayed in the air, they were so rickety." *Red Tails,* the major motion picture based on the stories of Tuskegee Airmen, the first African American military aviators in the United States armed forces, reminds Roberts of her father. Colonel Roberts, who served as a Tuskegee Airman in the US Air Force, was very humble as a lot of service men from his generation were. He didn't share war stories with Roberts or any of his children, but around the time the original Tuskegee Airmen movie aired on HBO in 1995, her father became more vocal about his experiences.

After seeing *Red Tails* in 2012, she felt the film was an extremely true portrayal and she loved that the movie was not about victims—it was about heroes. Roberts appreciated how the director, George Lucas, didn't try to sweep under the rug all that these men went through and the racism they endured in fighting for our country. "I appreciated that and this is why my dad would never allow us to play the race card," Robin shares. On Good Morning America in 2003, Roberts had the honor of flying an AT-6, an Air Force training aircraft her dad once trained in. The production team posed the question: If you could do anything in the world what would you want to do? Robin replied, "I want to fly a plane like my dad did in World War II." They found an old clunker and Roberts joked that she wanted to fly a plane like her father did, not the *actual* 50+ year-old-plane that he flew in World War II. "This thing came chugging down the runway and my father was just beaming," Robin shares. "Some of my favorite video is of him watching me fly and being with other Tuskegee Airmen." Her dad told her, "I never felt more free than when I was in the cockpit. I never felt more free than when I flew." Roberts shared that after having that feeling of freedom it must have been very hard for her dad to return to civilian life and deal with the harsh realities of living in a racist America after that experience."

Knowing that her father came from humble beginnings and went on to fulfill his dream of becoming a pilot influenced her to pursue her own dream of becoming a sports journalist. "It was almost like, how dare I not try to do this. My father, who had nothing, went on to do extraordinary things in his life and when we look at the generations of blacks that came before us with very few rights and even fewer resources. How could I not go for it? How could I not try?" Robin shares. Her father's life and the examples he set, dared Roberts to reach as high as she could to pursue her own passions. Her dad, through his actions and his commitment to giving his very best to his work and his family, taught her that with everything she did she should put forth her best effort.

During times when Roberts has faced challenges in her career and even battled serious health issues, she has often heard her father's voice and gleaned some of the lessons he taught her. Colonel Roberts taught his youngest daughter how to use humor in the face of adversity. He taught her how to be diplomatic, how to talk to people, and how to use different skill sets to solve problems or resolve issues. Roberts's father was the master of persuasion.

Every day Roberts saw examples of a healthy relationship in her parent's marriage. Even though her parents were very different, they complemented each other. She absolutely loved the yin and yang of her parents. Her dad, who didn't want to fall into stereotypes, would say to her mother, "I am not eating fried chicken or watermelon in public." Her mother, whom Roberts considered a "rebel," would look at him and reply, "Are you kidding me? Well pass the chicken to me 'cause I'm eating it!" Her dad was very conservative, and her mom, though she never drank alcohol, smoked cigarettes or cursed, was just the opposite—hence the yin and yang that she appreciated about her parents. Lucimarian, who, sadly, passed away on August 30, 2012, possessed a fun-loving spirit. She had a big laugh and a big smile. "What I love about their relationship is that my mother in essence put her life on hold for my dad and her children," Robin says "Once my dad retired, it was almost like he said, 'Okay honey, it's your turn." Lucimarian became a Gulf Coast icon for more than four decades and went on to serve as the first black chairman of the Mississippi State Board of Education in the 1980s. She also had a great passion for poetry and music. Once it was her mom's turn to chase her dreams, Colonel Roberts was then the spouse who stood by his wife's side and hung out with the other spouses. Roberts appreciated seeing how her father took a step back.

In her eyes, her parents' marriage was the definition of a true partnership. Despite the fact that they had their problems, she witnessed her mom and dad work really well together. Her mother once talked about how after Roberts was born she wanted out of the marriage. They had been traveling and moving for many years and made the decision to retire in Tuskegee. They had put down money on a house, and Colonel Roberts went behind his wife's back and changed his mind, which made Lucimarian furious. Colonel and Mrs. Roberts were by no means Ozzie and Harriet, but the thing that always brought them together was their mutual love of God and family. "This really helped them in those times when I'm sure they both thought about leaving," Robin admits. "I mean, can you imagine? You're in your twenties. You're living in Japan of all places. You've got a baby. You've been married a year, and you have no one around you. It's amazing that they did so well in all these years of marriage." In the end, their children could tell they were good friends.

Roberts fondly remembers her parents' fiftieth wedding anniversary celebration held at her home in Connecticut in 1997. Honoring a longtime tradition, the family gathered together in a prayer circle at the end of what turned out to be a wonderful day. Colonel Roberts began the prayer, and his voice cracked, which was a huge deal to Roberts because her father was showing heartfelt emotion—something he didn't readily do. He was moved because he and Lucimarian had everyone together celebrating such an important milestone—his son and daughters, his grandchildren, close family members and friends. As her father looked around the room, he talked with sincerity about his life and their marriage. Celebrating this important anniversary with his wife and those he loved, in his daughter's home on such a beautiful day reaffirmed to Colonel Roberts that he had accomplished all that he wanted to accomplish in his life. He was profoundly moved.

Roberts and her parents often traveled together. Their last family trip, shortly before her father passed away, was to South Africa. The family spent time in Johannesburg and Cape Town, visited Robben Island, and went on a safari. She recalls how at one point during the vacation her mom forgot her camera in the hotel room. She and her dad had to walk quite a distance to go back and get the camera. Her father was out of breath while walking and Roberts remembers thinking with concern, "Well, that's not like Daddy." Colonel Roberts took a few minutes to catch his breath, and he didn't want his daughter to tell anybody that he was having difficulty. "We had this glorious trip, and he passed away a couple of months after that at the age of eighty-one," Robin shares. "My dad saw me become the news anchor, but he passed away before I became an anchor at Good Morning America. He passed away shortly before I became one of the anchors with Diane Sawyer and Charlie Gibson," Robin says. "I so wanted him to see this, but the comfort I have is that I know my father was proud of me and that's the only thing that I, or any child, could ever ask for. She believes he accomplished many of his dreams, the biggest of which was of flying planes. The fact that he flew bombers and scrambler jets, and took part in three wars—World War II, The Korean War, and Vietnam—tells the story of his tremendous heroism. In addition, he was incredibly proud that all four of his children were responsible, college educated, law-abiding citizens.

The most important thing Roberts wants the world to know about her father is that he was good man, a good father, and a good husband. He was someone who always wanted to do right and he was so proud of his country and proud of his people. He taught his youngest daughter that she couldn't fail. Failure was not an option for the Tuskegee Airmen because they knew how far it would set the country and African Americans back. Roberts carried that lesson with her when she was hired by ESPN as the first black female sportscaster and sports anchor. In the back of her mind she realized that if for whatever reason she blew the opportunity or if she failed, a major network would be far less likely to ever hire another black woman. "It's not fair, but that's just how the world is," Robin says. "And my dad never played the race, gender, or any other card. That's the simple, yet beautiful thing about my father. There was nothing grandiose about Colonel Lawrence Roberts. He was just a good, good, good man."

Reverend Nicholas Hood III

Minister and Community Leader

"My father is a loving person and a tremendous role model in that he loved each of his kids uniquely."

Walking in faith and following Christ's example of love, service and humility are two roles Reverend Nicholas Hood III embraces each and every day. This extraordinary man is many things to many people—pastor, husband, father, brother, son, spiritual mentor and friend, to name just a few. To his congregation, he is a fearless leader who uplifts, inspires, and encourages by practicing what he preaches. The power of his ministry lies in the fact that he doesn't preach from on high. Rather, he rolls up his sleeves and works to find solutions to everyday problems faced by thousands of Detroit residents while creating ways for the community to put God's teachings into practice. Thankfully, Reverend Hood never had to go far to find a shining example of a man who walks with Christ and lives a purpose driven life. All he had to do was look into the eyes of his own father, Reverend Dr. Nicholas Hood Sr., to understand what it means to serve as a living, breathing example of

God's love. Like his father, he lives by the words of Jesus, "To those whom much is given, much is required."

After graduating from Wayne State University in 1973 with a degree in economics, Reverend Hood earned a Master of Divinity degree from Yale University in 1976. He returned to Detroit to work with his father as associate minister of the Plymouth United Church of Christ. After an eight-year tenure as associate pastor, he was called to be the senior pastor in 1984, where he serves presently. Under his pastoral leadership, Plymouth is a progressive church with a biblically-centered, relevant interpretation of the teachings of Jesus with a mission to serve the wider community in the areas of housing, education and mental health by giving members of the community a hand up, not a hand out.

His father, Dr. Hood, is the youngest of eight children, born in 1923 in Terre Haute, Indiana. The elder Hood met Elizabeth Fleminster in New Haven, Connecticut when he was a Yale Divinity School student and a youth worker at Dixwell Congregational Church. Elizabeth was a member of his youth group and a student at Albertus Magnus Catholic College in New Haven. They married in 1949.

Dr. Hood's father, Orestes Hood, was an electrician by trade and a distributor of a popular box radio called the Fader Radio. When the Great Depression hit, his inventory was worth less than what he paid for it, and he sunk quickly into financial ruin, alcohol, and deep depression. Seeing his father go through such a difficult time was one of the most traumatic experiences of Dr. Hood's life.

To make matters worse, Dr. Hood developed scoliosis, a severe curvature of the spine, and spent a year after high school on his back in a body cast. Once he was able to walk again and lead some semblance of a normal life, he was so grateful to his doctors that he considered becoming a doctor himself so that he could help others.

Dr. Hood enrolled in a local college and later transferred to Purdue University in West Lafayette, Indiana where he worked two jobs to help pay his tuition. At the time, the student body at Purdue University was comprised of approximately 6,000 white students and twelve black students. Although eligible for admission, black students were not permitted to live in the dormitories. Instead they were placed in a building called the International House, which was the only building that blacks could live in on campus. The students slept in the unheated attic of the International House.

Dr. Hood lived in this separate and unequal housing along with A. Leon Higginbotham, the future civil rights advocate and federal appeals court judge appointed by President John F. Kennedy to the Federal Trade Commission, making him the youngest and first African American to ever serve on a federal regulatory commission. Dr. Hood and Higginbotham became founding members of the Rho Sigma chapter of Omega Psi Phi Fraternity and Dr. Hood became one of the first African American students to graduate from Purdue University.

While Dr. Hood was studying at Purdue, his father learned of a job opportunity at Purdue for electricians and came to campus to interview for the job. The gentleman conducting the interview was

Dr. Hood's supervisor. When the supervisor found out that the job candidate was Dr. Hood's father, he said, "If you are Nick Hood's father, that's good enough for me." It was the work he found at Purdue that allowed Orestes Hood to once again earn a decent income and get back on his feet.

Dr. Hood got to know the chaplain on campus who encouraged him to think about the ministry and consider going to Yale Divinity School. He had never heard of Yale and still held an interest in medicine. He told the chaplain, "I'm a poor guy. How do I go there?" The minister, who had attended Yale himself, saw great potential in him and helped him secure a scholarship for disabled students to attend Yale Divinity School. In 1949, Dr. Hood graduated from Yale Divinity School, the same year he and Elizabeth were married. The young couple hopped a train for New Orleans where he was called to minister at the Central Congregational Church in an area of the city by the projects, just north of the French Quarter. Two years later, Dr. Hood and Elizabeth welcomed their first child, Nicholas III, into the world followed by three more children, Emory, Sarah, and Steve.

In 1958, Dr. Hood received a call to lead the Plymouth United Church of Christ in Detroit, Michigan with an annual salary of $5,000. He decided to take the offer and moved his family moved to Detroit, where he became very active in the life of the community. In a six year span, he became the second African American elected to the Detroit City Council in the last century and gradually worked his way up to become president.

As a child, Nick Hood III watched his father grow in the ministry and also in Detroit politics. He remembers his father being a busy, yet wonderful dad. He can recall his dad, a preacher who grew up poor, being very cost conscious. Even though Reverend Hood cannot remember his father eating dinner with the family, he remembers his dad preparing breakfast every morning like a short order cook. Whatever the kids wanted he would make. When they ran out of food, his father would get creative. He would serve toast and leftover meat, and he would make gravy. His father forced all of the kids to drink juice out of small Dixie cups. Hood surmised that this stemmed from his father growing up very poor during the Great Depression. "That's what he knew," Nick says.

Hood described his father as a disciplinarian, and though he wasn't mean, he believed in corporal punishment if the Hood children got out of line, which wasn't often. When Hood was nine years old, his father was shaking hands with congregants after Sunday service as they passed from the parish hall into the lounge. Two older ladies were walking at a slow pace to greet his father. Unbeknownst to Dr. Hood, his son brought a snub-nose squirt gun to church. The ladies' rear ends were right at eye level. He surreptitiously pulled out the squirt gun and took dead aim, wetting their Sunday's finest in front of the whole church. His father took him to the kitchen and, as Hood described with laughter, whipped him with the janitorial broom, much like a public flogging.

As a child Hood played organized football and baseball. He had to walk at least a mile and a half to practice, but during games he would look out in the stands and without fail he would see his father sitting there cheering the team on. To this day he remembers the feeling of seeing his father support him and each of his siblings children in everything they pursued.

Throughout most of his life, Hood's first passion was music. He played in bands in high school and thought he would surely become a professional musician. His band, "The Seven Sounds" played Detroit's local hotel circuit including the historic Book Cadillac Hotel and the St. Regis Hotel. They also played parties hosted by young African American social organizations and had gigs at the local union halls where they made a lot of money. His father and sometimes his band mate's father would drive the young men to their gigs. On Saturday nights, his dad would drop them off at eight o'clock to set up their equipment. The band would begin at nine and play until two o'clock in the morning.

Dr. Hood would pick them up an hour later after they broke down their equipment and take them back to the west side of the city to drop off their equipment. They would sit until four in the morning at the famous Esquire Delicatessen eating corned beef sandwiches. Dr. Hood was with them the whole time, and it wasn't until Nick was much older that he realized what a hardship this was on his preacher father who had to get up and preach on Sunday mornings. His dad always told Hood that taking the band members to their gigs was comforting for him because he knew where they were on Saturday nights, and he could work on his sermons between dropping them off and picking them up.

Hood greatly admired his father for having this perspective and learned a valuable lesson about what being a committed father meant. His father told him years later how happy he was that he got music out of his system. His dad feared that he would become a professional musician. While he wanted his oldest son to pursue his dreams, he was concerned about music not being a stable profession. He was also afraid that his talented son would have to face the unsavory conditions of playing in bars and living on the road.

One of the greatest lessons Hood learned from his father was that he tried to give each of the four Hood children what he thought they needed. Dr. Hood was elected to the Detroit City Council in 1965 and re-elected in 1969 just as the younger Hood graduated from high school. He spent the summer of 1969 campaigning for his father. Late that summer, Hood caught a plane to Boston to begin his freshman year at Boston University. His father gave him a plane ticket, a blue trunk for his clothes, a footlocker, a set of directions, and a couple of dollars. He recalls his father and mother coming to visit him in Boston only once, two months after he arrived on campus. Conversely, when Reverend Hood's other brothers went to college, his father drove them to school and made sure they arrived safely and helped them settle into their dorm rooms.

"You didn't drive me to school, why is that?" he asked his dad one day.

His father, a busy minister, and City Council member replied, "I didn't think you needed it." Dr. Hood went on to explain that every one of his kids got what they needed.

Hood's younger sister, Sarah, was stricken at age two with a severe illness. She suffered from a stroke that rendered her incapacitated. Prior to the stroke, Sarah could walk on a limited basis, but she could never really talk. Her severe disabilities and her diminished quality of life were very disheartening to the family, especially their mother. His father decided to create what Nick referred to as "contraptions" for his sister. He disassembled the light in the middle of the basement, installed a fishing pole, and had Sarah in a makeshift device where he would walk her in a circle. Until the age of fourteen, Sarah stayed at home where Dr. and Mrs. Hood had someone with her at all times. After a lot of prayer and hand wringing, they decided to make Sarah a ward of the state, believing she would get better treatment in a facility with a dedicated medical team. The Hood men would get Sarah from Plymouth State Home every weekend just to spend time with her. In the mid-1970s, Dr. Hood secured $250,000 in funding from the Kresge Foundation for a partial day activity center for the developmentally disabled. The center was named the Cyprian Center after Sarah Cyprian Hood. Years later, Hood's dad explained that he got the funding for the Cyprian Center when he and his band were playing a gig at the Cranbrook School, an exclusive private school located in the Bloomfield Hills neighborhood. "While you guys were out there playing, you thought it was so hard on me because we were so far away and it seemed like a long way back home," his father said. "The Kresge people were all there because that's where their children went to school, and I was busy working the crowd. By time you got through playing I had the money for the Cyprian Center."

Hood's younger brother Emory, a bright young man who played the bass guitar in the band, had a drug problem that started in the ninth grade. His addiction got really bad when he was a junior at Michigan State University where he was arrested for selling marijuana. Hood remembers his dad pouring out his heart for Emory. He tried everything to help him, putting him in program after program. Emory eventually went to jail where the family would visit him. The sadness and stress of having a disabled child and another child with a drug addiction took a toll on Hood's father and mother. "My parents kept moving but it really hurt them," Nick admits. "To this day, every now and then my dad will ask, 'what did I do wrong?'"

Hood remembers one evening when his father called him around midnight and said, "Man, I want to go find Emory." Nick agreed to go along. His father picked him up in his city-issued, red Grand Fury. They swung into a busy White Castle restaurant parking lot looking for Emory. Emory didn't show up until two in the morning looking disheveled. Hood and his father shoved Emory in the car and took him home. Hood didn't realize until years later when he was on the Detroit City Council himself that city-issued cars are marked, and the police know exactly who drives them. "We were sitting in a den of drug activity and here's a dad jeopardizing his career for his kid," Nick says. "Even though my father was not selling or doing drugs, the place was infested with drugs, and he was willing to do what he had to do to get his kid." Sadly, Emory later died of a drug overdose at age thirty-six and Hood's sister, Sarah, also died to soon at age thirty-one.

During Hood's second year of college, he flew back to Detroit two weekends out of each month from Boston University to perform with his band. He did the math and figured out that everyone in the band was making money except for him because all of his money was spent on airline tickets. Much to his mother's chagrin, Hood decided to transfer to Wayne State University to give his music career a real go and see if the band could land a recording contract. His mother was mortified that he would leave Boston University to pursue a music career, but his dad said nothing.

When he came home to enroll at Wayne State and play in the band, his dad asked if he would help him build a youth ministry for junior high school kids. Back then the church had a well-established high school ministry, but they didn't have a junior high program. Hood agreed to work with his father, and by the time he reached the end of his music career at the age of twenty-one, he had found his calling in the ministry, which he slowly discovered was much more fulfilling than the music. "That was the surprise I never dreamed of," Nick explains. "I found out that by the time I was ready to graduate from college, the ministry made more sense and because I had good role models in the ministry, people like my dad and Former Ambassador Andrew Young, I knew I could do this with my eyes closed."

After graduating from Wayne State University in 1973 with a degree in economics, Hood followed in his father's footsteps and went to Yale Divinity School. His first day on campus, he met Denise Page, a lovely Yale undergraduate student from Ohio. In addition to the joy he felt meeting his future wife, the young minister remembers having such a positive experience at Yale. He was the second director of the Yale Gospel Choir and essentially rebuilt the choir using his music expertise. Hood also had a positive experience working with his pastor at the student-run black church at Yale. During his last semester, his father asked him where he planned to work after her graduated and suggested that he come to work for him for two years. After graduating with a Master of Divinity degree in 1976, his father took a chance on him and gave him a job. Dr. Hood explained that it would take him five years to learn the job but encouraged him to come for two years to see how he felt about the experience. In two years he would have church credentials under his belt and maybe a church would extend a call to him. "That was the agreement," Nick says. "Two years morphed into many more, and I have been there for thirty-six years. I have to credit my dad because he was very good at identifying leadership. He identified me as a youth leader when I was in college and then came back years later and asked me to come work at the church."

It goes without saying that the parallels between Reverend Hood and his father are uncanny. Both father and son graduated from Yale Divinity School, both have served as renowned pastors, both are considered pillars of the community and both were upstanding members of the Detroit City Council. The younger Hood, while proud to walk in his father's footsteps, had no plans to run for City Council until one day when two of his father's preacher friends, whom he suspects his father may have "encouraged," took him to lunch at a very fancy restaurant. The preachers explained that they wanted him to think about running for City Council. Initially he said, "No, that's my dad's thing, I've never had any desire to run and furthermore, if I ran for office people would think I was running on my dad's name."

One of the gentlemen had a very interesting response: "You know, the bible says a good name is better than riches. Think about all of the young men who are ashamed of their fathers, all of the young people who don't even know who their fathers are, or all of the young people whose fathers are an embarrassment." The friend continued, "There is nothing embarrassing about your father. He has a good name, and he's given it to you. You shouldn't be ashamed of that. You should carry on the tradition." Hood thought about it and decided maybe they were right. He ran for City Council and served for eight years. "It was a good experience, and I have no regrets," he says.

Looking back on his father's years of service on the Detroit City Council, Hood remembers going to some of the early black political meetings. At a young age he learned about the infrastructure of local black politics in the Randora Hotel, where he met some of the most influential politicians in the city. He appreciated that his father thought enough of him to expose him to the inner workings of the political power structure and gave him insight into what politicians thought of Detroit's political future. Because his father essentially allowed him to witness history in the making, Hood thought it was important to take his own sons to political meetings when they were very young. He and his wife, the Honorable Denise Page Hood, welcomed their oldest son, Nathan, into the world when she first ran for judgeship in the 36th District Court in the state of Michigan. They would take the baby to political meetings because they knew that everyone loved babies, and women, young and old, wanted to hold him. He remembers passing his newborn son from person to person, and remarked that between birth and his college graduation Nathan got sick only once.

In 1993, Hood was elected to the Detroit City Council and was reelected for a second four-year term. He recalls that as a City Council member he took his young sons with him to the public forums. He would sit them in a corner during the meetings where they would do homework. "Everybody wins from this," he says. "No television, no distractions, just a bunch of old folk they don't want to be around and I had my eye on them the whole doggone time." Though it's still too early to tell, Hood believes his youngest son, Noah, may have political interests. He has had the greatest foundation in politics. Since Noah was a little boy, Hood has taken him to political meetings. And in his eight years on the City Council, Noah spent all but one summer at what his dad dubbed "Camp City Council" where Noah would pack his toys and spend the day with his dad in his chambers. "Noah got to see political people as they are—very, very human. He had nicknames for all of them," Nick recalls. In 2001, Hood stepped down from the Detroit City Council to run for mayor. Although his run for Mayor was unsuccessful, his campaign energized many in the city to envision a community of prosperity, inclusiveness, and unparalleled quality of life.

Hood's parents were married for over forty years at the time of his mother's death. He recalls that his parents sometimes had disagreements, but his father thrived on his mother's intellectualism because he had someone he could really talk to. Elizabeth appreciated her husband's intellectual side as well. Elizabeth was a linguist who spoke French, Italian, Spanish, and Portuguese. She earned her PhD from Wayne State University, where she later became a tenured professor. At one point after she wrote her dissertation, she wanted to take the core of the dissertation and put it into a book. Dr. Hood decided to self-publish the book. He found a printer to print a couple thousand copies of her book, which she titled, "Educating Black Students." He created NESS Publishing, which stood for Nick, Emory, Steve, and Sarah. Dr. Hood didn't know how they would sell the books but decided to contact every library in America to pitch the "revolutionary new book." He sold every copy.

Elizabeth was diagnosed with multiple myeloma and passed away more than twenty years ago. Dr. Hood lost his partner of more than forty years and their two remaining adult children, Nick and Steve, lost an extraordinarily committed mother. As painful as it was to let her go, Dr. Hood surrounded himself with the love and support of family and friends. A few years after Mrs. Hood's death, he met and married Doris Chenault, a retired Detroit public school administrator. Dr. Hood, now eighty-nine, and Doris have been married for eighteen years.

Reverend Hood has learned a lifetime of lessons on how to be a devoted husband, father, and pastor from his father's tremendous examples. There are a few things, however, that he approaches differently, including his stance on punishing children. As he grew up spankings in the Hood household were few and far between, he learned from them. He made a commitment that he would never whip his own children. When his sons were old enough to understand, he explained to them that when they get out of line, he wouldn't hit them. He would simply talk to them. And talk he did—until he was blue in the face. "You know, there were a couple of times when the kids would beg me to hit them just to get it over with," Nick says with a look of parental satisfaction. From his perspective, it requires a greater challenge to discipline children without beating them. He believes it is the easiest thing in the world to haul off and hit someone. However, to Hood, taking the time to intellectually engage children and getting them to understand why you are displeased while letting them know you love them is a far greater challenge that yields long-term rewards.

From his father, who has always been respectful of people regardless of social and economical circumstances, Hood also learned to respect and communicate with others – no matter their status in society. He has tried throughout his life to let others know that he loves and is respectful of all people regardless of how much money they have, or don't have. The most important thing Reverend Nicholas Hood III wants the world to know about his father is that Dr. Hood is a loving person and a tremendous role model in that he loved each of his kids uniquely. He did not try to be fair or equal. Instead, he loved each of his four children individually and gave them exactly what he thought they needed.

Russell Simmons

Cultural Icon and Master Entrepreneur

"My father was pretty laid back... He was a man of culture, an artist and a poet. He gave me a roadmap by example and he was cool, that's why I wanted to be like him."

Although it may be hard for some to believe, cultural icon Russell Simmons didn't arrive at this staggering level of success and affluence on his own. He didn't just wake up one morning as one of the most innovative and influential figures in modern American business and culture. With the roll of the dice, he didn't just turn into an international human rights advocate, champion of the Occupy Wall Street Movement, and stalwart animal rights activist. Quite the contrary, he absorbed the good and the bad from his surroundings. He strategized, planned, and meditated. Simmons created a vision and a path to enlightenment that fueled his staggering success. His undeniable sense of self came from watching, listening to and learning from his father, Daniel Simmons Sr. Russell Simmons's tireless advocacy in strengthening race relations and promoting tolerance and understanding is an enduring testament to his father.

Simmons has been the authority in bringing the powerful influence of hip-hop culture to every facet of business, media, and fashion. The master entrepreneur, with an estimated net worth of $340 million, has been in the business of creating an entirely new, post-racial, progressive new America. Simmons's business success has always been rooted in giving a powerful voice to emergent new creative and social movements, and integrating them into the American psyche. His father's wisdom is at the core of all that he has achieved.

Born October 4, 1957 to Daniel and Evelyn Simmons, Russell was raised in Hollis, Queens, a middle class neighborhood of New York. His older brother, Daniel Simmons Jr., is a famed abstract expressionist painter and his younger brother, Joseph Simmons, or "Reverend Run" of the legendary rap group, Run-DMC, is an ordained minister and a reality television personality.

Simmons's father grew up in Baltimore, Maryland. From the time he was old enough to engage in real dialogue with his father about life and manhood, he and his dad talked at great length about the elder Simmons's upbringing and how tough it was growing up on the crime-laden streets of Baltimore. Daniel Sr. told his son stories of how he wouldn't back down, refused to do what the "cool" people did and was never, ever a follower. "He wasn't a punk and he was always tougher than everybody because he did what he wanted to do," Russell says.

Simmons's father was a well-read poet and an artist who valued education. Education, he believed, was a critical component of success. The younger Simmons describes his dad as a "cultured man." "You know, he was a big cultural kind of guy. He wrote poetry. He could recite all of Shakespeare's stuff and he knew all kinds of African American history so he was a renaissance man in many ways," Russell says. Simmons describes his father as a very outspoken activist and a servant others would look to for leadership. Daniel Sr.'s leadership qualities can certainly be attributed to his upbringing but he inherently gravitated to specific ideas about the whole of humanity and mankind. Ultimately he believed he was on this earth to make other people's lives better.

Both of Simmons's parents attended Howard University. The elder Simmons worked for the New York Board of Education as a public school administrator and a senior truant officer. He was also a history teacher and later in his career, he became a professor of Black History at Pace University in New York. Simmons remembers with pride that his father accomplished a great deal in his life and was particularly proud to teach Black History. By and large, Simmons thinks his dad left an important legacy for his kids and grandkids. He believes that a lot of his dad's dreams were not only embodied in his work as an artist, a poet and professor, but also in his *being*—Daniel Sr. was satisfied with his life and seeing his kids achieve so much meant a lot to him.

In addition to being an educator, the elder Simmons was a passionate student of black history. He became an educated civil rights activist and yet he remained "real," priding himself on staying connected to the streets. Daniel Sr. often talked of bourgeoisie black people who became educated and purposely separated themselves from the reality of people on the ground. He was indeed empathetic to the plight of African Americans, yet he never supported the idea that by becoming elevated and enlightened, black people must disconnect themselves from the consciousness that the struggle takes on. Simmons draws parallels between his father's life and the life of a rapper. He recalls that like rap artists, his father wrote and recited poetry that may have been offensive to a lot of the upper-class, black bourgeoisie. Above all else, Simmons's father inspired each of his sons by being connected to the streets and the suffering of black people in America.

Simmons speaks poignantly about his father, juxtaposing his connection to the streets with a sense of culture that allowed him to exist between two worlds. Simmons thinks about the poetry and the art that his father cared about and notes that his father prided himself in embracing the hood without being consumed by it. He went on to explain that his dad did not respect black men who go along with what's not threatening. He deplored the idea of living to simply exist. He remembers his father, who passed away in 2006, as a revolutionary. As such, Simmons spent years cultivating his own sense of self, taking social and cultural cues from his father and paying homage to the legacy Daniel Sr. left behind.

Simmons credits his father as the person who shaped his views in terms of seeing the world through the lens of true individualism and making choices in his life that were not conventional. "Do you.

Don't be a follower. Don't be a sheep," Russell says, remembering what he learned from his father. Simmons argues that most young people do a lot of things just to be cool. In fact, in his first attempt to become a successful entrepreneur, he sold marijuana and later, fake cocaine, which he made from crushing up coca leaf incense. In his book, *Super Rich*, he wrote, "I responded to the low notes that were playing around me with some of the things that I did earlier in my life." Admittedly, he fell prey to the trappings of society, trying to wear certain clothes and do things others did. But while Simmons had his share of missteps, he kept his eye on the "cool dudes" on his block—the educated ones. He saw educated black men as inspirational. Like his father, they motivated him to succeed and let him know that if he worked hard and created a roadmap for himself, he could one day have a life that far exceeded his own expectations.

Neither his father nor his mother was much in the way of being strict disciplinarians. However, when Simmons or his brothers did something their father didn't like, "he whipped that ass," Russell admits. Approval from his dad was a pat on the shoulder. Simmons remembers his dad being pretty laid back throughout much of his childhood. He provided all three of his sons a roadmap by example and, Simmons will never forget that his father was a trendsetter. "My father was cool, and that's why I wanted to be like him. He'd have a funky hat. I would rock his hat. My father was more connected to me in a friendly way more than a disciplinarian, angry way. He would lead me rather than dictate," Russell reflects.

Teaching Simmons and his brothers about earning and saving money was not much of a focus for his father, although he managed to teach them more about finances than their mother did. Russell recalls saying to his mom, "I have 114 college credits and I need two more credits to graduate, but I'm gonna drop out of school and go promote these parties and produce this music." His mother's reply: "Oh good! Here's some money, go do it. Here's the rest of your college money." Russell laughs as he recalls this exchange with his mother. She, too, was a true artist who encouraged freedom and promoted happiness over worldly pursuits. Simmons feels that his mom knew he was smart enough and that ultimately he was doing what he wanted to do.

Daniel Sr. and Evelyn raised their sons together until they separated toward the end of Simmons's childhood. Rev. Run, seven years Simmons's junior and the baby of the family, was impacted more by the separation than his older brothers. Rev. Run lived with their mother after their parents' separation but both parents remained extremely involved and influential in all three of the boys' lives. Despite their split, the Simmons brothers shared a good amount of quality time with their father. Russell contends that each of the Simmons boys learned important lessons about manhood from their father, but the most important lesson was their father's encouragement to be an individual. From his father, he saw positive examples of what it meant to be an individual every day. This sense of individuality is the very fiber that makes Simmons who he is and informs all that he has worked to build as a businessman, activist, and enlightened yogi. "I think that a fundamental flaw in our education system is the way parents sometimes rear their children in that we're taught to follow what it says in the book," Russell says. "I was taught to question what was in the book." His father never stifled his creativity or his dreams. He allowed Simmons to think for himself.

At a young age, Simmons saw how his father lived his life and prided himself on being *in*, not *of* the community. Although Daniel Sr. didn't promote disdain for the norm or the "black establishment," he always poked holes and exposed them. In a very similar vein, Simmons took on a very public role of bringing national attention to the Occupy Wall Street Movement, the people-powered resistance movement that began in 2011 in Manhattan's Financial District. The Occupy Wall Street Movement has spread to over 100 cities in the United States and over 1,500 cities globally to fight back against the major banks and corporations over the role of Wall Street in creating an economic collapse that has caused the greatest recession in generations.

As an international human rights advocate, Simmons often feels that the rights we as Americans are fighting for are no good unless we extend those rights to others. "African Americans in particular often believe that we're victimized, and we accept it," Russell says. "Instead of giving credence to the suffering of others we focus on and accept our own burdens and lick our own wounds." Like his father, Simmons has a broader sense of the world and relates the suffering of people in our community to the suffering of others.

Simmons espouses the belief that even when people are encouraged to be individuals, just as he and his brothers were, personal discipline is part of the inspiration because as individuals we still have a higher calling. He believes that there must always be balance. "You have a smarter being that's separate from you that sits inside of you that you are always digging for. Self-interest or self-study is important. The idea of sumati as the yogis refer to is about self-study, so you have to have that perspective as well. The Buddha would say, 'Check for yourself,' forget what the prophets and the books tell you and find out what you think for yourself. It doesn't mean that he doesn't give you a prescribed path because there is not a prescribed yogi path to enlightenment. It just means that a most critical part of it is self-study." Simmons's father instilled in him the idea of self-study. "He didn't teach me to meditate, he taught me to respect the process—the value of self— because he always was an individual. He was a poet. Poets have that, artists have that," Russell says.

His father reminded him of a preacher in that he was a great and powerful speaker. Daniel Sr. was a Christian, but he was not a deeply religious person, and his spirituality was based in compassion. He was not a philanthropist in the purist sense, where he gave money to promote the welfare of others. The elder Simmons was, however, into promoting civil rights, which by Russell's estimation, is a profound gift to the universe and philanthropic in its intent. His father's view of politics was all about helping the underserved.

Simmons experiences many moments in his busy life as a human rights and animal rights activist where he draws upon his father's wisdom. "I always hear my father's voice. He's always there," Russell reflects. "Whether it's a discussion about art, the N-word, or people's unwillingness to look at real things and have their own perspective versus being sheep. When I say 'Oh, we lost over 3,000 people and my people were killed in the bottom of the World Trade Center" but 400,000 Iraqis were killed, and they're innocent as well, and you know, we never discuss them. Or when I talk about how people are so unconscious about the fact that innocent people around the world are bombed. Even when I'm talking about animal rights or that 40 billion animals are born into suffering, it's my father that gave me that." Daniel Sr. inspired his oldest son to fight for what he believes. "Whether it's the gay rights work that I do, the civil rights work, the support of Occupy Wall Street, fighting for other people, that is in part my father—all of that came from my father."

His approach to parenting is similar in principle to that of his father, and he is thankful that his ex-wife, Kimora, is a great disciplinarian, which leaves him the space not to be. Simmons is passing fundamental values that celebrate individuality and compassion on to his daughters, thirteen-year-old, Ming Lee and ten-year-old, Aoki Lee. He reminds his girls often of human suffering and many of the lessons he learned from his father. Simmons says he talks with his daughters all the time about his work and how his father inspired him to become the person he is today.

The most loving memory Simmons has of his father is the moment his dad winked at him the day before he passed away. "I remember that being kind of a statement. My father was saying, 'I'm okay,'" Russell says. "That meant a lot to me, and it was a moment of great encouragement for me to let go of fear. It was very helpful to me." Simmons wants the world to know that his father left a tremendous legacy and shared with him and his brothers, very valuable lessons. "Our inspiration comes from our father so if there's anything that's done by my brothers or myself, we have to acknowledge our father because that's where it came from."

Rosalind Brewer

Corporate CEO

"Despite working three jobs, my dad came to every event and was present for every award I ever received. I don't care where it was, if I got an honorable mention I'd look out in the audience and he'd be sitting there. For all of my violin recitals and piano recitals, my father never missed one of them."

Rosalind Brewer is in the business of making history. She is the very first African American woman to hold the position of president and chief executive officer of Sam's Club, one of three major divisions of Wal-Mart Stores, Inc. and the nation's eighth largest retailer. Brewer leads more than 100,000 associates across 616 stores that generate close to $54 billion a year. She joined Wal-Mart in 2006 as regional vice president overseeing operations in Georgia. From 2007 to January 2012, she was division president of the Southeast before taking the helm at Sam's Club. Despite being one of the most powerful women in corporate America, it's her "realness," her approachability, and her outright brilliance that wins over skeptics who find it incredulous that a woman could achieve and sustain this extraordinary level of success.

Brewer serves on the board of directors for Lockheed Martin Corporation and is chair of the board of trustees for her alma mater, Spelman College. She was honored by *Fortune Magazine* in 2010 and 2011 as one of the fifty most powerful women in business and is on *Black Enterprise Magazine's* 2012 list of seventy-five most powerful women in business. As president and CEO of Sam's Club, all eyes are on this scientist turned corporate change agent. Brewer has a cadre of cheerleaders—from her family and friends to colleagues and fellow alumna of her beloved Spelman College. Loyal supporters are watching her every move and praying that the wind is at her back as she takes Sam's Club to higher heights. As an African American woman in this highly visible role, Brewer understands that to succeed she must remain true to the core values she learned growing up and the lessons from her father, George Gates, that have informed many of her life decisions.

Brewer's father was born in 1929 in Bessemer, Alabama where he lived until he fled the South after being falsely accused of making a pass at a white woman. Brewer recalls talking with her dad about racial incidents that he and his eleven siblings endured, particularly the three male children in the Gates family. His mother, fearing that she would one day find one of her sons hanging from a tree, shipped all three boys out of the South when they were roughly eighteen years old. George went to live in Gary, Indiana where he worked in the steel industry. After a couple of years he moved to Detroit while he looked for work in the burgeoning auto industry. He moved into an apartment building with his first cousin where he met his future wife, Sally, and found a job with General Motors. George and Sally married in the 1950s and had five children. Rosalind, born in 1962, is the youngest of their children.

Brewer described her father as an extremely talkative, very handsome, bright man. She recounts how she and her siblings always got "the lecture" from their father, who loved to teach his children lifelong lessons. If one of the kids came home for lunch on the rare occasion that he happened to be home on his own lunch break, without fail they would be late getting back to school because he would find something to lecture them on—from their musical interests to what he was reading in the newspaper that day.

Her dad was very supportive if ever she had trouble in a class or with a teacher and wasted no time going up to the school to talk to the teacher. "He would show support, but if he got up there and found out you were acting out or it was your fault and you blamed the teacher, you were due for a spanking, plain and simple." He would let his kids know in no uncertain terms when he wasn't happy. "It's funny, parents know their children and their needs better than anyone else," Brewer says. "My dad knew I was a little more independent because I saw the way he treated some of my other siblings that needed a little more coddling than I did. So he would respond to them in that way." In retrospect, her father was probably a little tougher on Brewer because he thought she could take it. At the time Brewer thought it was harsh, but she believes he may have seen something in her. George watched her grades carefully and knew that she had quite an aptitude for math and science. He encouraged her to do her best and thought that she could possibly go into engineering. He had high expectations for his daughter's future and they talked about it often.

George believed in the old adage that kids should be seen and not heard. She and her siblings were not allowed to participate in conversations until he felt they were worthy. To Brewer, the conversations her father would have with them were absolutely wonderful. "He was such a teacher," Rosalind says, glowing. George taught his children how to interact with people and how to treat people. "He could walk in the room and everyone would fall in love with him." Brewer's dad was a Christian man who studied the bible and liked to get into intellectual debates with members of the Jehovah Witness religion. He would even invite the Witnesses into the living room where they would debate and discuss the bible for hours.

Her father never finished high school and really wished that he had gone to college. Brewer heard her dad talk sometimes of a desire he once had to go to medical school and become a physician. He also talked about how he could have done something different at General Motors if only he had a college degree. He clearly wanted a different kind of future for his children and did not want them to follow in his footsteps, which is why he taught them to focus heavily on education.

In 1967 when Brewer was six years old, the family moved to the Northwest side of Detroit. Her parents bought the home from a

Jewish family and for many years the neighborhood stayed racially mixed. For at least ten years the Gates family had as many white neighbors as they did black neighbors, most of which were physicians and teachers. She recalls that her father built additional rooms in their house, something he taught himself how to do. He would read, learn, and then teach. What he lacked in formal education, he more than made up for as a self-starter with a tremendous amount of drive.

As she grew up, her father talked with her about hard work and shared stories of how his own father worked in the coalmines, which means George didn't get to see him much. George did odd jobs as a child to help with all of the kids in the household. He felt very responsible for his nine sisters and served as their caretaker. When he grew up and had a family of his own, he taught his children to genuinely appreciate family. Brewer jokes that growing up she couldn't tell her first cousins from her siblings because if any of them went away to the Army, for example, they would come back to see her father first before going to see their own parents. He would sit and talk with his nephews, "schooling" them on manhood. "He was outstanding in that way," Rosalind says.

George lived what he espoused and had incredibly high expectations for all of the young people in his life. He not only told them, he *showed* them every single day what real fatherhood and hard work looked like. At one point, four of the Gates kids were in college at the same time. He worked three jobs to pay for his children's education, and Sally worked as well. In addition to his job at General Motors, he sold real estate and worked at Hiawatha Construction. He also played the saxophone in Detroit nightclubs. He had no formal training, just a love for music. When he began to move up into management at General Motors, where he ran warehousing and distribution for the Cadillac facility and the Fischer Body plant, he was able to leave the other jobs behind. Brewer remembers that her father held a pretty big logistics position at the time of his death and was still working when he passed away from colon cancer at the age of fifty-four.

Despite putting in long hours, Brewer's father came to every school event and was present for every award she ever received. "I don't care where it was. If I got an honorable mention, I'd look out in the audience and he'd be sitting there," Rosalind says. "I was the youngest of five and he was present at all of my violin recitals and piano recitals. He never missed one of them." This show of love from her father is indelibly stamped on Brewer's heart. It made her feel a huge sense of responsibility because she felt like someone was always watching, that someone cared—and that someone was her father. His absolute presence in all areas of her life, from the grandest school plays to the smallest violin recitals, made her raise her standards because her dad was going to come regardless, and she realized the sacrifices he made to show up to each and every event. Above all, she wanted to make her father proud.

Brewer's parents worked so much that to her, their relationship felt like a marriage of convenience. She doesn't recall seeing a whole lot of affection between her parents, but the feeling in their household was one of amicability. Simply put, they were two hardworking parents running a household. George worked days, and Sally worked nights on the line in an auto manufacturing plant her entire career. Brewer remembers the auto industry having tenuous times and her father being worried about not having a job. Somehow he always made it through, particularly when he got into management because those most impacted by layoffs and budget cuts were the hourly employees, not necessarily management. She recalls times when money was tight for their family, and yet her dad insisted on sending money back to his family in Alabama until he died. To him, family was everything.

While she remembers the hard times, she wasn't fully aware of her parents' financial struggles because there was always food on the table. She recalls never eating fast food or even canned vegetables until she was in the eleventh or twelfth grade. Food was always fresh in their home and the family sat down together to enjoy a big Sunday dinner each week. Despite financial struggles, Brewer remembers never really wanting for anything. Once she got into high school and wanted designer jeans, her parents made it happen. She knew it was a sacrifice for them to provide these kinds of things for her and her siblings. Each of the Gates kids was appreciative for everything their parents did for them and showed it.

Brewer has been gainfully employed since she was sixteen years old. She worked in the evenings after school, on Saturday mornings, and in the summers. Once she started driving, it was her responsibility to pay for auto insurance and gas. Her summer jobs helped her meet these obligations. Her father would remind each of the kids of the importance of looking out for each other. If one didn't have something, he would want the others to help their brother or sister. Brewer remembers when her sister, who is several years older, helped her purchase a dress for the high school prom. "That's just the way we were," Rosalind says. "We always took care of each other."

Each of Brewer's siblings went to college in Michigan, and Brewer believed she would continue the tradition by enrolling in a local engineering program. Because neither her father nor her mother knew how to complete a college application, she relied on her older siblings to help her navigate the process of selecting, then applying to schools. Like her father, her sister, Sandra, saw something special in her and encouraged her to leave Michigan for college. Brewer decided she wanted to attend Spelman College in Atlanta, and when she and Sandra presented the idea to their parents, they were supportive and thought it was a fine idea. She left for Atlanta in 1980 to begin her four years at Spelman. During her freshman year, she met a fine young Morehouse man, John Brewer from northern California. Rosalind and John began dating sophomore year. During this time her father was diagnosed with cancer. He passed away just two years later in March of 1984, two months before Brewer graduated with a degree in chemistry.

Though losing her father was one of the most difficult times she would ever face, Brewer pressed on in a way that would have made him proud. She accepted a job offer from Kimberly-Clark, starting as a scientist in nonwoven technology and product development before becoming president of the Global Nonwovens Sector in 2004. Brewer continued her education by way of the advanced management program at the University of Pennsylvania's Wharton School of Business.

Upon accepting the position as CEO of Sam's Club in February 2012, Brewer has commuted every week between Arkansas, where Sam's Club is headquartered, and Atlanta, where she has lived with her husband of almost twenty-five years and their two children. The family plans to join her permanently in Arkansas soon. Despite her hectic work and travel schedule, the CEO takes every opportunity to spend time with her family. "So far so good," Brewer says of the weekly commute. She tries very hard to make it to her son's varsity baseball and basketball games and her daughter's soccer games. Her kids know that they can count on her and they value their nightly chats with their mom via Skype. She spends time talking and laughing with them and although they are almost 500 miles apart during the week, her commitment to her kids is 100% non-negotiable, as was her father's commitment to her. Both Brewer and her husband have purposely put a lot of time into their children. "The reason John and I have such a great relationship is due to our sense of family," Rosalind says. "He was raised by his very strong father, and he got a chance to meet my dad before he passed away so my husband gets it."

As she has ascended through the ranks to one of the very highest positions in corporate America, Brewer has thought a lot about her father and the lessons he taught her. She feels that her dad would be absolutely beside himself to see the level of success she has achieved. Her position as the president and CEO of Sam's Club she believes would have far exceeded her father's expectations. "In actuality, the day I left for Spelman to start my first year of college did it for my dad. A college education was his wildest dream for all of his kids. "The level of success I have achieved as an executive," Rosalind beams, "I think would be breathtaking for my father, and I try each and every day to honor his legacy and make him proud."

Ilyasah Al-Shabazz
Motivational Speaker and Author

"While traveling in Africa my father wrote, *'My journey has almost ended, and I have a much broader scope than when I started out, which I believe will add new life and dimension to our struggle for freedom, honor and dignity in the United States.'* I carry this important message in both my heart and in my mind. It feeds my spirit and fuels my passion for honoring my father's life and uplifting his legacy."

Proud, tall and regal like her father, with a radiant smile and sincere eyes that resemble those of her mother, Ilyasah Al-Shabazz, the third of Malcolm X and Dr. Betty Shabazz's six daughters, is an extraordinary leader in her own right. To his admirers, Ilyasah's father, Malcolm X or El-Hajj Malik El-Shabazz, was a prominent figure in the Nation of Islam who articulated concepts of race pride and Black Nationalism until the time of his death in 1965. Malcolm X was known by many as the man who revolutionized the black psyche, becoming one of the greatest and most influential African Americans in history. To Ilyasah, he was known simply as "Daddy."

Shabazz's presence fills the room the moment she enters. Her presence, however, is eclipsed only by her intellect and her desire for people of color to know themselves and understand their history, and for the world to understand the significant contribution of Africa and the Diaspora. While Shabazz, who reads and writes Arabic, continues in her parents' immense footsteps, she in no way stands in their shadows. She is an accomplished author, motivational speaker and producer who has traversed the United States and the world over to promote peace and to advocate for human rights and social justice. Shabazz is trustee for the Malcolm X Foundation and the Malcolm X and Dr. Betty Shabazz Memorial and Educational Center, Inc.

The brilliant woman who carned a Bachclor's degrcc in biology from State University of New York and a Master's degree in education and human resource development from Fordham University did not get the chance to grow up in the protective arms or under the watchful eye of her father. Shabazz's understanding of her father, a public figure that loomed larger than life on the world stage of international human rights and American civil rights, came directly from her mother who very privately preserved his legacy as a proud father and family man. It wasn't until Shabazz went to college that she began to fully grasp the magnitude of her father's public persona and develop her own identity as the daughter of Malcolm X.

Shabazz's father, a courageous advocate for the rights of African Americans, those of the African Diaspora, and those oppressed regardless of ethnicity, religion or gender, was gunned down at the height of the civil rights movement on February 21, 1965 at the Audubon Ballroom in New York City as he prepared to address the Organization of Afro-American Unity in front of 400 eyewitnesses including his wife, pregnant with twins, and their four young children. Shabazz was not yet three years old when her world was turned upside down. Still, she reflects on her father's prodigious impact on her life and the values set by both of her parents—values that her mother continued to foster and reinforce in each of the Shabazz girls after their father's untimely death. To her parents, it was important for her to understand what it means to be a woman, a Muslim, and a person of the African Diaspora. It was also important that she learn to embrace the lessons of service and the meaning of living a purpose-driven life.

Shabazz readily points out that many people loved and deeply respected her father but they forget that he was very young, just in his twenties when he changed the narrative for African Americans in the fight for social and economic equality. As she speaks to groups around the world, she reminds men and women who loved her father that Malcolm X was a leader in the movement for only twelve short years when his life was taken at age thirty-nine. She reminds his supporters of her father's legacy and his brilliance. She talks of how he read everything one could imagine by or about people of color—including newspapers, magazines, biographies, the classics, African history, and the origins of religion.

Malcolm X was born Malcolm Little in Omaha, Nebraska on May 19, 1925. Ilyasah candidly reflects on her father's life, intellectualizing the impact his parents' lifestyle and his upbringing had on his chosen path—from his misguided decisions to embrace the life of a street hustler that landed him in prison, to the power of his convictions that shaped the future for African Americans. "His father, Earl Little, and his mother, Louise Norton Little, were well-read, well-educated citizens who promoted literacy, accountability, responsibility and leadership ideals in their children," Ilyasah shares.

Malcolm's mother, Louise, originally hailed from Grenada in the British West Indies. An educated woman, Louise spoke five different languages and held the position of recording secretary for the Garvey movement, named for Marcus Aurelis Garvey's Universal Negro Improvement Association. Garvey commanded millions of followers worldwide in the 1920s. He raised the banner of black-race purity and exhorted the masses of blacks in America to return to their ancestral African homeland—a cause that arguably made Garvey the most controversial black man on earth.

Malcolm X's father, Reverend Earl, standing six feet five inches tall, was a Garveyite activist from Georgia who served as a dedicated organizer and officer in Garvey's organization. According to Shabazz, Earl and Louise met in Canada at a Garvey rally. "My grandfather helped to get Garvey released from prison for alleged mail fraud in the 1920s. He brought his young son, Malcolm, with him to rallies and meetings." Because of Earl's stance on freedom and independence for black people and his prominent position in the Garvey movement, Louise felt the threat from the Black Legions, a local hate society, who on several occasions came to their home brandishing shotguns and rifles. The Black Legions harassed the family, busted the windows out of their home, and tried to scare Minister Earl into silence.

Fearing the worst, Louise rallied the support of her fellow Garveyites and local West Indian families, asking that they raise her children with the values important to her and her husband if something should happen to them. Minister Earl refused to be intimidated. On two occasions, their homes were burned to the ground and they were forced to move from Wisconsin to Nebraska, then to Lansing, Michigan, where the white supremacist group eventually killed Minister Earl. "My grandfather was assassinated for gathering names on a petition to bring the United States up on charges before the League of Nations, the predecessor organization to the United Nations, for trampling the human rights of African Americans," says Ilyasah. "The story is that they hit him over the head, tied him down onto the train track, and waited for the train to run him over."

Eventually, local authorities stepped in to seize the family's land, placing Louise in an institution and sending the Little children off to three different families. "Clearly, when you have two conscious activists as were Earl and Louise, you ensure that your children are equally conscious and equipped to be leaders in the movement for social justice. Earl passed the baton to young

Malcolm," says Ilyasah. "He was following in the footsteps of *his* father and once incarcerated and introduced to a religion that enforced pride in his heritage, he was able to reflect on similar values instilled in him by *his* parents. My grandfather was preaching the same message that my father later preached, which was a message of independence, self-love and self-reliance. This was considered a threat to white supremacy," Ilyasah intimates. "A lot of people aren't familiar with this story. They think Malcolm rather evolved miraculously out of nowhere."

During happier times, Malcolm X's mother made sure that her children read newspapers to her while she ironed clothes and cleaned the house. She also made sure they read the dictionary from cover to cover, completed their studies, and engaged in meaningful dialogue about life. During times of the economic depression, Louise made sure her children cared for the livestock on their land and that they understood, whether an insect, animal or human being, it was important to have compassion. Young Malcolm and his brothers and sisters were taught to respect and appreciate life. When Louise was placed in the State Mental Hospital in Kalamazoo, Michigan, her children were sent to live with family associates. Malcolm was eventually sent to a foster home in Lansing, Michigan.

Malcolm X, who showed signs of brilliance at an early age, had dreams of becoming a lawyer. He was always passionate about the justice system and, as a young boy, understood some rudimentary aspects of American law. Unfortunately, a white teacher told him that practicing law was no realistic goal for a nigger. He found himself drifting from wanting to be his best to having no dreams at all, and moved to Boston to be with his elder half sister. In Boston, Malcolm got into petty crime, eventually dropping out of school altogether and ending up in jail. "After his mother was taken away, without proper guidance my father was lured into the streets," Ilyasah says. "Ironically, he was still a genius in the streets."

Shabazz's mother, Betty Shabazz, was born Betty Dean Sanders May 28, 1934 in Georgia to young, unmarried parents, Ollie Mae Sanders and Shelman Sandlin. Betty, raised in Detroit, was a young nursing student when she was introduced to Malcolm X at the mosque in New York City. Betty was teaching health and hygiene at the mosque and Malcolm was a minister who also loved art, history and poetry. There was an immediate connection between Malcolm and Betty. They got to know one another by engaging in great discussions while strolling about museums and art galleries. The young couple married January 14, 1958, in Lansing, Michigan. Betty gave birth to six children, Attallah, born in 1958; Qubilah, born in 1960; Ilyasah, born in 1962; Gamilah Lumumba, born in 1964; and twins, Malikah and Malaak, born in 1965 seven months after their father's assassination.

Malcolm X, as a husband and father, was very sentimental, especially when it came to his "Apple Brown Betty," as he adoringly called his wife. He loved her beautiful brown skin and wrote for her poetry. Malcolm appreciated beauty in the little things that made his life with Betty special. Theirs was a loving, old-fashioned relationship where he would leave money for his wife so she could go shopping to buy some of the things she loved. The Muslim leader and charismatic speaker loved his wife for her wit, self-reliance, compassion and loyalty. He appreciated that she understood how difficult the break from the Nation of Islam was for him in 1964.

Malcolm and Betty's home was fire bombed on Valentine's Day in 1965, and Shabazz recalls stories of her father being completely incensed, particularly because the firebomb was thrown into the nursery where his children were sleeping. "It was one thing to want to kill him, but to want to harm his babies and his wife, you know that's when reality set in," says Ilyasah. "I mean he was human and he was so young, only in his thirties."

After Malcolm's death, Betty received an outpouring of love and support from her relatives, celebrity friends including Sidney and Juanita Poitier; Ossie Davis and Ruby Dee; and a host of people who cared for Malcolm and their young family. Betty made raising the girls her single most important mission and although she was left exhausted caring for the physical, emotional and financial needs of six children, Betty never, ever gave up or gave in. Ilyasah and her sisters were never made to feel that were raised in a single-family household because their mother kept their father's spirit and message very much alive in their home. After his death, Malcolm X's personal belongings were always present in their home—his briefcase, coat, hat, many of his papers and his books were there for his daughters to see and touch. At dinnertime when the girls would sit around the family table talking about the day's events, Betty would speak lovingly of their father. She would talk about their shared values and lessons that he would have passed on to his daughters. "Daddy wouldn't agree with that, he would do it this way, or Daddy said this," Betty would say.

Shabazz holds on to memories of seeing her father's face, touching his hands and hearing his voice. She also remembers the special blue and white rocking chair that her father gave her before the house was fire bombed. She discovered that she shared a love for cookies with her dad. During the holidays each year, her friends gave her cookies, cookie jars, or anything related to cookies. Her mother told her the story of when her father was alive, Shabazz, then just a toddler, would run to the front of the house waiting to see her daddy walk through the door. In anticipation of Malcolm coming home, Betty often made his favorite oatmeal cookies. He would walk through the door and tenderly kiss his wife and daughters. Betty would hand her husband a plate of warm cookies, a glass of milk, and many newspapers and periodicals. He enjoyed the cookies and milk in the den while watching the evening news.

After his death, the family stayed at the home of Sidney and Juanita Poitier. Shabazz carried on her ritual of going to the door of the Poitier home and peering curiously out of the window, waiting to be swept into her father's arms. Betty later shared the story that she didn't know how to tell a toddler about death so she would put her daughter's favorite cookies on a plate and break one in half for her. The cookies symbolically became Shabazz's crutch and a welcome distraction for a young girl missing the first and most important man she'd ever love.

Shabazz has no recollection of the day her father died. Her mother never talked about his death because it was too painful. Betty never visited Malcolm's grave and she was overprotective of her children who were forced to go through life without a father. She kept them busy with boarding schools and prep schools. Shabazz went to summer camp in Vermont, and then to her grandmother's house in Philadelphia before the school year began each year. Outside of school, the Shabazz girls were involved in yoga, dance, music, art, and history lessons. Betty purposely kept her daughters immersed in educational and creative environments. "There's this thing my mother would always say: 'Find the good and praise it.' After my father's body was placed in the ground, my mother never talked about any of the trauma; she only talked about the good memories," says Ilyasah.

As she grew up, Shabazz understood her father's impact but as the sheltered child of Malcolm X and Betty Shabazz, she didn't witness his vulnerabilities or experience just how much of himself he sacrificed. As a child, there was no way for her to understand that her young father must have been frightened at times when he confronted hate, bigotry and an overall lack of consciousness in the fight for social and economic equality. Shabazz began to grasp the magnitude of her father's legacy when she went to college. During her freshman year, she read *The Autobiography of Malcolm X* for the very first time as a young adult and took a class about his influence during the civil rights era. Other students would run after her on campus asking, "Are you Malcolm X's daughter? Are you Malcolm X's daughter?" Her newfound enlightenment while simultaneously being thrust into the spotlight was overwhelming. "I read the autobiography in my dorm room and I just remember it being a very emotional experience," says Ilyasah.

Shabazz has always been close to her mother and is so very proud of all that her mother, who lost her life in 1997, accomplished and all that represented to many single parents. Betty raised six girls while furthering her own education. She earned a Master's degree in health administration in 1970, and in 1975 she defended her dissertation to earn her doctorate in higher education administration and curriculum development. She went on to become a tenured professor of health administration at Medgar Evers College—and ultimately the college's cultural attaché. Betty spoke publicly at colleges and universities about the philosophies of Malcolm X. She also spoke about her life as the mother of six beautiful girls and the wife of the extraordinary human rights leader.

Betty's life and legacy inspired her daughters and the many, many people who loved, respected and admired her. "My mother was so much fun. She was candescent, fashion-forward, compassionate, loving, she was wise, she was beautiful and she was nurturing," says Ilyasah. "As children, we believe that all these great qualities in our parents are universal—you think when you go out into the world out from underneath the protective wings of your parents that everyone is like that. When you discover that's not the case, it really makes you appreciate the people who nurtured you."

Shabazz talked with her mother about any and everything—from her relationships to her feelings of being confronted with her own identity as Malcolm X's daughter when she went to college to identifying solid girlfriends and potential mates of the opposite sex. Betty always gave Ilyasah and each of her daughters the best advice she could possibly give. "I remember telling my mother that she was the most important person in my life," says Ilyasah. "My mother told me that *I* have to be the most important person to *myself* because I have to love myself first and foremost and not compromise my values based on someone else's love or opinion of me. I would imagine that's what she was able to bring about in her relationship with my father—self-love and knowing who she was and the values she would not compromise. And I'm grateful that she instilled those kinds of values in me."

Shabazz's relationship with her mother—and the lessons from her father that her mother passed on to her—taught her that as children of God, we all have a purpose in life. She believes both of her parents were extraordinary role models and she doesn't believe this simply because they were her parents. Five years after her mother passed away Shabazz wrote *Growing Up X*, which is largely a tribute to her mother and chronicles her life from her father's death to her mother's death. In writing the book, she took the opportunity to really look at Malcolm and Betty as individuals. Seeing two young people through a different, more mature lens and understanding all they endured and all they contributed was a tremendous moment in Shabazz's life. "My mother witnessed her husband's death on February 21, 1965. Their home was fire bombed on Valentine's Day, a week prior to my father being killed," Ilyasah says. "My mother, still in her twenties, was left widowed, terrified, homeless, penniless, harassed, and a single parent now of four babies and pregnant with twins. This woman refused to accept defeat or limitations. She would never accept 'no' or 'I can't' as an answer for herself or her six daughters.

She became a role model for single mothers, and this just goes to show the power that we possess. She went on to earn her PhD, by driving once a week from New York to Amherst, Massachusetts with six babies at home. She could have gone anywhere but, like my father, she ultimately chose a position to serve others and was steadfast in her commitment to social justice," says Ilyasah. "My mother once told me, 'just as one must drink water, one must give back.' Being able to still go on and give and live, and accomplish all of the things she accomplished with six babies, I felt was such an inspiration that I wanted to share that story with others who felt challenged by so many different things in life, or who felt victimized."

In her wonderful memoir, *Growing Up X*, and whenever she speaks in a public forum, Shabazz describes her dad as compassionate, fair, gentle, loving, humorous, very sensitive, and an extraordinary problem solver. "The public image of Malcolm was always seen from the perspective of someone reacting to the social climate that already existed. To contribute all of your life's work to addressing the injustices of a nation really says a lot about a person," Ilyasah says. "It says something about one's integrity, compassion and commitment. It wasn't like he was doing these things to make money. He was doing these things out of sheer concern for the world, and black people in particular." To truly carry on her father's legacy, Shabazz believes that it starts with understanding that we can't expect other people to do for us what we have the power to do for ourselves, and if we understood history we would know that nobody is going to give us anything. "My mother and my father are both such inspirations to me. They influenced how I live my life today and always," Ilyasah says.

"While traveling in Africa in 1964, my father wrote something very profound to a friend that Ossie Davis, shared at his funeral: *'My journey has almost ended, and I have a much broader scope than when I started out, which I believe will add new life and dimension to our struggle for freedom, honor and dignity in the United States.'* I carry this important message in both my heart and in my mind. It feeds my spirit and fuels my passion for honoring my father's life and uplifting his legacy."

Andrew Jackson Young, Jr.

Civil Rights Activist and
Former United Nations Ambassador

*"My father taught me that God has a purpose for everybody's life.
You cannot tell somebody else what God's purpose is for them—
they have to find that out within their own souls."*

Imagine a time and place when a black man could stand strong and negotiate a racially charged incident with the power of his words and conceivably his fists—if it came to that—but not the life-altering destruction of a firearm. Imagine a generation of men that possessed a philosophical understanding of Christianity and human rights and created social change in an America that tried her best to reject all notions of equality for people of color. Those who lived during the civil rights era surely remember when leaders were *leaders*—purposeful, selfless and driven, not by personal gain, but by a higher calling.

Ordained minister, diplomat, politician, activist and humanitarian, Andrew Jackson Young, Jr. is one of these extraordinary leaders who has dedicated his life to helping write an egalitarian account of history for scores of black folks in an era when inalienable rights were inalienable for everyone but them. Young has established a brilliant legacy of servant leadership but as with any genuine leader, he didn't come into prominence on his own. His father, Andrew Jackson Young, Sr., a dentist by trade and a loving husband and father, helped him develop the blueprint for his own greatness. Young has served as Mayor of Atlanta, a congressman from Georgia's 5th Congressional District, and United States Ambassador to the United Nations. He served as President of the National Council of Churches USA, an influential member of the Southern Christian Leadership Conference (SCLC) during the 1960s civil rights movement, and was a supporter and friend of Dr. Martin Luther King, Jr.

His father, Dr. Young, standing just 5 feet 4 inches tall and weighing 140 lbs., was small in stature, but his love for his family was enormous. A good father and a good man in his son's eyes, Dr. Young was always ready and willing to take on the world. Fortunately for us all, he passed this zeal and sense of purpose on to his son. Both father and son are examples of extraordinary men who brought pride, intellectualism, compassion, and moxie to their respective generations and their respective callings.

Dr. Young hailed from Franklin, a small city in St. Mary Parish, Louisiana, just a little over 100 miles from New Orleans. He met his future wife, Daisy Fuller, when they were both students at Straight College. "Straight College was founded by the United Church of Christ, the same network of educational institutions that created the colleges in South Africa where Nelson Mandela received his education," explains Andrew. "Thus, the connection with Africa was made for me almost before I was born." Andrew has held a lifelong interest in Africa and has championed the creation of a shared vision and cooperative approach to development across the continent of Africa. He was a prominent figure in the United States campaign against apartheid and has been recognized for his friendship to South Africa and his exceptional contribution to the struggle against racism and apartheid.

Young's mother, Daisy, grew up in New Orleans. She was very righteous, an advocate of monogamy and faithfulness. After graduating from college, Daisy became a schoolteacher at a time when women teachers were not allowed to marry. Dr. and Mrs. Young were engaged for six years before they married in 1931, and according to Young, his mother would not sleep with her future husband until they were married. Young was born in 1932, and the couple's second son, Walter, was born in 1934. Both Dr. and Mrs. Young come from proud stock and held very high morals and Christian standards. The relationship between Young's parents was open and trusting. There wasn't a trace of jealousy between them even with male and female friends visiting the house on a regular basis. Young's mother had male friends and liked to play bridge. His father was a sports fan who often went to prizefights and baseball games. He didn't want to take his attractive wife to sporting events. The crowds were usually pretty rowdy, and Dr. Young didn't want anyone cursing and swearing around Daisy. Much to his chagrin, there wasn't much he could do about the rowdiness of the crowds, so he took his boys to the prizefights instead. He also arranged for Andrew, Jr. and Walt to go to the gym with the boxers to learn how to box. He would tell his sons, "If you know how to fight, you don't have to fight. It's only when you're scared of fights that you have to fight."

Dr. Young's dental office was located in the front of the Young family home in a middle class New Orleans neighborhood. They had neighbors from Irish, Italian, and German descent, and according to Young, "the Nazi party was on the corner where we lived." Even before Young went to school, his father had to explain what white supremacy meant and why people hollered "Heil Hitler!"

When Young was four years old his father took him to see Jesse Owens in the 1936 Olympics in Berlin and showed him that like Jesse Owens, being the absolute best at whatever you set your mind to was the way to deal with white supremacy. His father explained that Jesse Owens never got angry or upset about the blatant discrimination he and other black, world-class athletes endured. Instead, he went out on a track and proved that white supremacy was not true. Dr. Young told his son that white supremacy is a sickness as racism is a sickness, and that getting mad with sick people is futile. Instead, it was their responsibility to help them overcome their sickness by fighting not with weapons, but with the power of their words, their minds, and their will. His father also taught him that when you are in a fight, if you lose your temper, you lose the fight. His father drilled these messages into

Young's head from the time he was just three years old. Paradoxically, Young's grandmother would tell him that if someone picked on his younger brother or called him a nigger and he didn't do something about it, he was going to get whipped when he got home. He was smart enough to balance these lessons from two of the handful of people he cared most about in this world.

Young feels that he had an almost ideal childhood because he had two loving parents, and because his maternal grandmother and paternal grandfather were also heavily involved in his life. His maternal grandmother, Louisa Fuller, was a very religious woman who understood the importance of education. She had five children of her own and raised eleven children altogether. Whenever anyone in need came knocking on her door, she always felt she had a place for them. Louisa lost her sight when she was eighty years old. Young was just six years old at the time. His job was to read the newspapers and the bible to her. She taught him many things but one lesson that stuck with him was not to be afraid of death. Every day she asked God to take her home because she was ready to go on to glory. Louisa also told him every day for eight years, "You've been blessed, Boy. To whom much has been given, much is required." He took his grandmother's words to heart.

Dr. Young taught his son to respect himself and to make people respect him. Young would go downtown by himself on the streetcar when he was just six years old to the dental supply company for his father. His father always made him dress up in a shirt and tie. He was adamant that young black boys walking around downtown or in a store would be accused of stealing even if they were doing nothing wrong, but if they wore a shirt and tie it forced adults, particularly white adults, to respect them a little more. His father also taught him that he mustn't ever tell lies.

Dr. Young made every attempt to be a firm disciplinarian but Young managed to talk his way out of most of his whippings. His father used to whip him with a razor strap but one day when the future politician was ten years old, he stood up to his father. "No, you're not going to hit me anymore!" Andrew exclaimed. He left the house and ran down the street. Dr. Young came after his strong-willed son. Once he caught him he told the boy that he wouldn't hit him because he was so mad, he might hurt him. Dr. Young told his son that if he didn't want to be whipped, he must listen and be obedient. Young's mother, on the other hand, could never whip him. When he misbehaved, Daisy would send him to get a switch, and then he would start negotiating with her. "Momma, you don't want to do this. You say it hurts you worse than it hurts me. I know I'm wrong but I'mma do better." Young would run in circles around the kitchen table talking to his mother while he ran from her. According to Young, all of his whippings were the result of something his brother did and blamed him for.

One of his brother's typical tricks involved sabotaging their nightly dishwashing duties to get his older brother in trouble. Andrew's job was to wash the dishes and Walt's job was to dry them and put them away. After he washed and stacked the dishes,

Walt would announce that the dishes weren't clean and put the whole stack back in the greasy water. "Well, I slapped him and then my father and mother wanted to whip me," Andrew laughs.

The only real disagreement Young had with his father was about the profession he would choose for himself. As a teenager, Young read the poetic essay entitled, *On Children*, by Lebanese-American poet and writer, Kahlil Gibran in the 1923 classic, *The Prophet*. Young studied Gibran's timeless words:

> *Your children are not your children. They are the sons and daughters of Life's longing for itself. They come through you but not from you, And though they are with you yet they belong not to you.*

> *You may give them your love but not your thoughts, For they have their own thoughts. You may house their bodies but not their souls, For their souls dwell in the house of tomorrow, which you cannot visit, not even in your dreams. You may strive to be like them, but seek not to make them like you. For life goes not backward nor tarries with yesterday.*

> *You are the bows from which your children as living arrows are sent forth. The archer sees the mark upon the path of the infinite, and He bends you with His might that His arrows may go swift and far. Let your bending in the archer's hand be for gladness; For even as*

He loves the arrow that flies, so He loves also the bow that is stable.[2]

Gibran's writings made Young think deeply about his relationship with his father. He loved his father unconditionally, but he would not let his father control him. Dr. Young wanted his oldest son to walk in his footsteps by becoming a dentist and a baseball player, as he once was. Instead of going to dental school, like his father and later, his brother who went on to become a successful dentist, Young decided to answer a religious call that stirred in his soul. After earning his Bachelor of Science degree in pre-med from Howard University, he entered Hartford Theological Seminary in Hartford, Connecticut where he earned a divinity degree in 1955. While at Hartford, Young was exposed to the teachings of Mohandas Gandhi and became enamored with Gandhi's philosophy of non-violent social change.

Young expresses with humor that in some ways he failed his father because he did not become a dentist. When he was sworn in as Ambassador to the United Nations in 1977 under President Jimmy Carter's administration, United States Supreme Court Justice Thurgood Marshall said to his father, "You must be proud of this boy."

His father replied, "If he'd been a dentist, I'd be proud!" Although the elder Andrew had a great sense of humor, he was serious about not wanting his son to be a preacher. Dr. Young went

---

[2]   Gibran, Khalil. *The Prophet*. New York: Alfred A. Knopf, Inc., 1923. Print

to church every Sunday, tithed, sang in the choir and sat on the church board, but still believed all of the preachers he knew were either poor or crooked. He didn't want his son to be either. He proposed to send Andrew to any school he wanted to go to except divinity school. "If you choose to do that you will have to go on your own," he told his son. "I'll pray for you, but that's the best I can do."

"My father figured that if I became a dentist I could send my kids to college and live a secure, comfortable life as a community leader," says Andrew. "He didn't see any value and thought I was wasting my talents preaching."

When his father refused to pay his tuition to the seminary, Young didn't get upset but told him he would have to do it alone. Young left home and did not come back for over a year. He wrote his mother and father every week and his mother wrote him back, but Young did not come home for Thanksgiving, Christmas, or Easter. He was working and studying hard and believed this to be the best decision because it forced him to be serious about what he wanted to do. College was given to him and he "goofed off and wasted it," but Hartford Theological Seminary is where he got serious. He earned a scholarship and held four small jobs to help pay his tuition and expenses. He worked in the bookstore, washed dishes in the cafeteria, performed janitorial duties at an apartment building three blocks from the seminary, and served as youth director at a church on weekends. Ironically, he made more money and better grades at Hartford than ever before. While a student at Hartford, Young met his future wife,

Jean Childs. They married in 1954 and were husband and wife for forty years until Jean died from cancer in 1994.

After earning his divinity degree, he became an ordained minister in the United Church of Christ. He went to Thomasville and Beachton, Georgia to lead two little country churches with only fifty members collectively. With a wife and baby on the way, his salary was a mere $90 a month and he got $100 a month from the denomination. Despite his father's concerns Young felt he was doing just fine as a man of God.

Young's paternal grandfather, Frank Young, was the grand dictator and protector of the Knights and Ladies of Honor of America, a 10,000 member fraternal insurance organization. In August of 1932 at their annual convention, he reported that the cash assets for the organization exceeded $100,000. Frank was a man with only a fifth grade education. He was, however, a true savant with many interests. His occupations included mail carrier, insurance agent, and business owner. He was also a founding member and officer of the Louisiana Business League. Frank died when Andrew Young was just eight years old. He regrets not taking the time to ask his grandfather the questions he wanted to know about his life before he passed on. Gardner Taylor, known as the dean of American preaching, was a close friend and mentor to Martin Luther King Jr. and played a prominent role in the religious leadership of the civil rights movement of the 1960s. Taylor knew of the young congressman when he was a young preacher and when he met Young in Congress, he asked, "You Frank Young's grandson?"

Andrew replied, "Yes."

"Well, you're the first black congressman from the South since Reconstruction, but you still haven't done as much as your granddaddy did back before War World I."

Young held a tremendous amount of respect for his grandfather and could only laugh, shake Taylor's hand firmly, and reply: "The only reason I'm able to do anything is because of what my parents and grandparents did."

Whenever there was a racial incident in the town, his grandfather, a trusted member of the community, would go to the bank and demand to withdraw the fraternal insurance organization's funds of more than $100,000, instructing the bankers to transfer it to New Orleans or Baton Rouge because the white people in Franklin were not treating black people right. When the bankers were threatened with losing his money, they usually calmed the "hoodlums" down. This was an important lesson about fighting with power and resources that Young's father passed down from *his* father. Young was able to execute a similar strategy when the Ku Klux Klan came to Thomasville, Georgia. He had just gotten to the small southern town where he was running a voter registration drive with former Atlanta mayor Maynard Jackson's grandfather, John Wesley Dobbs. They had never seen the Klan before.

As they were driving back to Thomasville from Albany, Georgia, they came around the corner and saw a couple hundred people wearing sheets. Young figured they were coming to try to intimidate them about the voter registration drive. His first thought was if the Klan members came to his house he would go down and talk to them, but he wanted his wife to sit in the window with the rifle pointing at the guy he was talking to. He had been in seminary where they learned about negotiating from a position of strength, and Jean was taught nonviolence at Manchester College in North Manchester, Indiana, a school affiliated with the fundamentalist Church of the Brethren. Jean, a teacher who went on to become an acclaimed activist for civil rights, education, and children's welfare, refused. She said, "No, I'm not going to point a rifle at any human being."

Andrew replied, "That's not a human being, that's the Ku Klux Klan."

"Under that sheet is a child of God," Jean replied.

"Damn, woman!" Young's voice rose in frustration.

"If you don't believe that, you need to quit preaching and we need to go do something else," Jean said.

Young, joined by other black leaders, went to the Mayor to tell him the Klan was coming. The Mayor got on the phone with executives from Sunny Land Packing Company and Flowers Bakery, the two largest employers in the area, and it was decided that the Klan could meet and have their rally at City Hall, but they couldn't leave the county square, nor could they parade through the black community. The small town of Thomasville, Georgia got through this racial strife without a confrontation due in large part to Young's efforts. Lessons from Young's grandfather that his father passed down to him and the stubbornness of his wife reaffirmed for him that you can't be passive, you can't wait for them to come after you; you have to go after them in a constructive way using the power of your words and your mind. "This is what the Civil Rights Movement was all about," Andrew proclaimed. "We didn't wait for trouble. We went where we thought we'd find the best opportunity to create social change."

Young's mother was on the board of the Urban League, and his father was very active in the NAACP. But according to Young, Dr. Young didn't understand the civil rights movement. "My parents were what we call 'race people,' but nonviolent demonstrations and going to jail, all that sort of stuff, wasn't what they were about," Andrew says. Despite the fact that his father did not understand or embrace his civil rights work, he has led many organized protests where his father's wisdom guided his actions and his faith in God ordered his steps. He confronted segregation with Dr. Martin Luther King, Jr. and galvanized a movement that transformed a nation through non-violent resistance. Young was a key strategist and negotiator during the civil rights campaigns in Birmingham and Selma that resulted in the passage of the Civil Rights Act of 1964 and the Voting Rights Act of 1965. "Don't get mad, get smart," he could hear his father's voice. His father shared sage advice like, "You don't let anybody beat you down. You don't quit when you are in a fight. You keep fighting until you die. And if you're not afraid to die, then your opponent either has to kill you or respect you."

"I've been fortunate that I confronted people close enough and often enough that I got their respect before I got killed," Andrew reflects.

Young has received many awards and accolades for his selfless dedication to civil and humanitarian rights, including the Trustee's Emmy Award for Lifetime Achievement in 2011, presented by legendary television journalist, Tom Brokaw. Young doesn't personalize these honors and despite historical social change that has occurred under his watch, he believes that he is representative of many others. "I know the honors I've received are not mine," Andrew says. "They belong to thousands of people and I can't celebrate what we have accomplished because we, as a society, still have not delivered for the rank and file. The working class has slipped back and more of them are in poverty, black and white."

In reflecting on his life and the lives of those he loves, perhaps the most important lesson Young learned from his father—and also from his grandmother—is something he has passed down to his children and grandchildren: "God has a purpose for everybody's life. You cannot tell somebody else what God's purpose is for them; they have to find that out within their own souls," Andrew reflects. "You can give them examples or you can give them encouragement, but ultimately it's only as you search within the center of your own being that you know how God is leading you."

Denise Page Hood

United States District Court Judge

"My father taught us that you didn't get what you're getting on your own," says Judge Hood. "Lots of people are going to help you and you're not going to be able to thank all of them. Giving back is the way you thank people."

As we venture through this journey called life, we begin to understand that dreams evolve. This is especially true for many of our parents born during an era in which African American fathers often didn't have the luxury of chasing dreams of their own. For Richard Arlen Page, the father of United States District Court Judge, Denise Page Hood, what began as a dream of academic and professional pursuits of his own evolved slowly into dreams of being a good husband to his wife, Nancy, and a loving and present father to his two daughters, Denise and Teri. Though Richard Page departed this world more than a decade ago, Hood remembers her father fondly and recounts the close relationship they shared. She tells of the many ways her father's dreams were fulfilled as he worked tirelessly to create a loving family environment while encouraging his daughters to pursue opportunities that would allow them to grow beyond their own expectations. Richard Page believed there were no limits on how high his daughters could go in life. His lessons ignited in them both, a passion for education, a commitment to helping others and a sense of purpose.

As a wife, mother, federal judge and the first lady of Plymouth United Church of Christ in Detroit, Michigan, Hood has possessed a strong moral compass since she was a young girl— invariably thinking about her place in the world and how to make society fair and just. Deeply intellectual, compassionate and benevolent, today Judge Hood is a federal judge on the United States District Court for the Eastern District of Michigan. She was nominated by President Bill Clinton on March 9, 1994, confirmed by the United States Senate on June 15, 1994, and received her commission on June 16, 1994.

Her father, Richard, born in Columbus, Ohio in 1932, was the youngest of three boys. His father, Minister Thomas Nelson Page, Sr., instilled in his sons the belief that they had a responsibility to others. Richard, in turn, instilled this belief in his own children. "My father taught us that you didn't get what you're getting on your own," says Denise. "Lots of people are going to help you and you're not going to be able to thank all of them. Giving back is the way you thank people." These early lessons passed down from her grandfather, whom she credits as one of her greatest influences, set the foundation for Hood's own life and an unwavering sense of responsibility to others. To this day, whether she is presiding over her coutroom or spending time with her husband, Reverend

Nicholas Hood III, and two sons, Nathan and Noah, all Yale University graduates, Hood looks for the best in society and in others without judgement.

Born and raised in Columbus, Ohio, Hood is the oldest of Richard and Nancy's two daughters. Her father and mother, high school sweethearts, met at a church dance, attended the high school prom together and later married in 1951. Richard was from the east side of Columbus. Nancy hailed from the west side. Between their two large families, Denise and her sister, Teri, could be recognized anywhere in town as children from the Page and Penn families. It was *that* kind of community—roughly twenty-five percent African American at the time—where almost everyone knew just about everyone else. The Page girls were surrounded by love and knew that misbehaving with such a large extended family throughout Columbus would be a foolish proposition, though misbehaving was never really at the top of their agenda.

Hood always felt supported and protected by her father. Growing up, she knew he was there encouraging her, relishing the moments they spent together, admonishing her with a gentle yet firm hand when she got out of line, but always, always loving her. This feeling was something she never actively thought about, it just was. Her dad made it his priority to be there for her and her sister. He made sure they were able to be the best they could be, giving them things he never had as a child.

Richard graduated from East High School and attended The Ohio State University part-time. He had a warm, affable personality and a great sense of humor. He was quick to strike up a conversation at a party, the grocery store, or his daughters' school outings where he volunteered his time. Although a bit shy, Hood felt comfortable going anywhere with her father because he made friends everywhere he went. This always put her at ease. When Hood and her sister were young, Richard worked as a letter carrier for the United States Postal Service, as did his father and brother. Later, he went to work for the federal defense construction supply agency. Never afraid of hard work, Richard held several after-work jobs too. He worked nights as a custodian, for a department store in the paint and hardware supply area and he parked cars at a local country club during special events.

Growing up during the civil rights era when marches, freedom rides, boycotts and other forms of resistance to racial segregation and unfair treatment received national media attention, Hood was keenly aware that discrimination against African Americans existed. After all, this was the time when Brown vs. The Board of Education decision in 1954, the Civil Rights Act of 1964 and the Voting Rights Act in 1965 helped bring about the demise of the entangling web of legislation that bound blacks to second-class citizenship. Hood can recall times in her dad's work life when he expressed disappointment and felt the sting of racism as he and other black men were passed over for promotions and opportunities to earn higher wages. Her parents didn't, however, try to hide or sugarcoat these painful times. Instead, they moved through these teachable moments together as a family.

When Hood started fourth grade, her parents decided it was time to move from their apartment and began looking for a house. They looked at house after house in different neighborhoods throughout Columbus. When they drove past a nice-looking home with a 'For Sale' sign in the front lawn, the Page family would pile out of the car, walk together to the front porch, and ring the doorbell. They hoped— and expected—to be greeted with respect as they searched for a new home. On more than one occasion, white homeowners would come to the door with trepidation and immediately announce that the house had already been sold. The next week they would drive by the same house, and the 'For Sale' sign would still be there. It was obvious that the white homeowners would never entertain the idea of selling their house to a black family.

It was an early dose of reality for the young Page girls, and they learned first-hand that people would purposely do something or keep them from having something simply because they were African American. Richard and Nancy taught the girls that discriminatory acts were real and beyond their control, and that such acts had nothing to do with who they were as individuals. The family was not discouraged, however, and continued to look for a house in different areas of the city. As fate would have it, the neighborhoods they were turned away from were by no means better than the working class neighborhood where they ultimately bought their home.

Richard was an intelligent man who enjoyed talking about issues that affected the world. From culture to African American history, from sports to current events, he often engaged in discussions and debates with friends. He passed his inquisitive nature on to his girls and also encouraged their love of reading. When Nancy was ready to give birth to their youngest daughter, Richard drove the soon-to-be big sister to the library, which was just down the street from the hospital, to check out a book. Children weren't allowed in maternity wards so he seized the moment to do something educational to pass the time while they waited in nervous anticipation for the newest member of the family to arrive. Father and daughter sat in the car and read *The Collected Poetry of Paul Laurence Dunbar*. Though she wasn't quite four years old, this is one of Hood's fondest memories of the very special times she shared with her dad.

Her father was what Hood considered a "humorous disciplinarian." Growing up, she would ask him for something and he would say, "Go ask your mother" because he wanted and needed his wife's input. He felt it was necessary for them to be on the same page when making decisions. "When they weren't in agreement, it was kind of like a joke," says Denise with laughter. There were times when her father would threaten to whip her when she disobeyed. He would whip his belt out of the belt loops and snap it up in the air with a loud pop! In a firm voice he would say, "Go upstairs and lie on the bed. I'll be up to whip you in a minute!" She would wait upstairs for twenty minutes. Just the fear of her father whipping her was more terrifying than it actually happening. She can only remember one time when her father swatted her with a belt on the legs. "Hold still so I can whip you," he would say with great authority. "What planet is he from?" Hood recalls thinking, trying not to laugh at her father, whom she loved with all her heart.

Richard taught his daughters valuable life skills but managed to have fun along the way. He had been a lifeguard as a young man and wanted his daughters to become good swimmers and have respect for the water. One day while Hood was taking a swimming lesson she recalls her father bursting with laughter as the lifeguard stood at the very edge of the highest diving board and held Hood upside down by her ankles. She squealed with fear and delight, knowing that he held her securely in his grasp. The lifeguard insisted that she learn to dive into the pool headfirst in order to earn her next swimming badge. He warned her jokingly that if it meant he'd have to drop her, he would do just that. Hood remembers yelling, "Dad, save me!" but her father was too busy laughing at the lifeguard and knew that no harm would really come to her. She did in fact learn to dive into the pool headfirst, causing her to reflect years later on her father's unique ability to teach life skills in a lighthearted way as well as to expose his children to fun-loving situations that life sometimes presents.

On hot summer nights, Richard would occasionally announce to the girls that he was taking them to a drive-in movie while their mother worked. He instructed them to put their pajamas on and told them not to tell their mother about these special outings. After the movie, they would drive to pick Nancy up from work at midnight.

She would slide into the passenger's seat, lean in to kiss her husband and turn to greet the girls who were sitting in the backseat in their pajamas, smiling and happy to see their mother. The next day, little Teri would blurt out that daddy took them to the drive-in to see a movie. The three of them would sit there looking like mischievous kids caught with their hands in the cookie jar.

One day a terrible flood swept through central and southern Ohio. Richard said to his family, "Let's go out and see the flood!" The Hood girls thought it sounded like one of their dad's great adventures, but their mother knew the idea was insane. They drove out into a flooded area where, at one point, it didn't look like they would be able to get their car out of the water without being rescued. Richard, in his calm, good-natured way just chuckled as the car started to take in water from a hole in the floor. The girls pushed back the floor mats to see the water rushing beneath and splashing into the car. Richard and the girls thought the experience was hysterical. Nancy, on the other hand, didn't find it the least bit amusing.

Richard carefully balanced the fun and adventurous times with the more serious side of parenting, helping with homework and overseeing piano lessons while their mother worked in the evenings. Although Richard and Nancy married and had children at a young age, they were wise beyond their years and worked hard to provide discipline and taught their daughters the importance of planning and saving money. Hood readily admits that of the two, her mother was a better debt manager who felt that the family didn't need to take on debt of any kind. Her father, on the other hand, had a slightly different approach to managing the household finances. In the sense of being a good financial steward, he always had enough money to take care of the family, but Nancy thought her husband could be a bit frivolous with money, sometimes going out on a limb to pay for things they didn't necessarily need.

Education was the primary focus of the ever-evolving dream for his family. As both Richard and Nancy began to discover that good grades and being at the top of the class came easy to his daughters, Richard made sure both of his girls attended the best schools they could send them to, even if he had to figure out how to do that without necessarily having the means. He emphasized to his girls that there were limitations on money, but he never made them feel as though they were poor.

September of 1966 marked the beginning of Hood's freshman year in high school at Columbus School for Girls. She wasn't thrilled about going to an all-girls school where she would be one of seven or eight African American girls in the student body, but she had earned a scholarship, and Richard knew his oldest daughter would receive a good education that would prepare her for college. He reminded her that she wasn't going to the school to make friends, she was going to get the best education possible, and that as a ninth grader, she shouldn't expect more than that. Her father was, in that sense, very honest about the sacrifices the entire family had to make to fulfill this dream. He taught her the value of a world-class education and what people gave up to make sure they had a good academic foundation.

In the Page household, the children didn't get paid for chores or household responsibilities such as cleaning their rooms or getting good grades. They received praise, but not an allowance, because they were expected to do those things. When Hood was in the tenth grade, her father said, "You know, you need to go out and find a job." She got a job first as a babysitter, then as a waitress. Richard took her to open her very first checking account and showed her how to balance her checkbook every month. He also gave her tips on the best way to save for things she wanted to buy. The importance of these first job experiences weren't necessarily the jobs themselves, it was the fact that her father and mother made sure she understood that the money she earned belonged to her. After all, her parents tried to be quite pragmatic when it came teaching their daughters about the value of the dollar.

She began to feel a newfound sense of freedom and independence in high school and began going out on the weekends with new groups of friends. She was also introduced to the idea of dating, even if the dates happened in groups. Unbeknownst to Hood, her father decided it was time for him to show up in places he was least expected such as the bowling alley she frequented with a group of friends. Soon, everyone knew her dad was bound to drop in to see how the teenagers were behaving. "They would say, 'Page, your dad is here!'

People began to think he was an undercover cop and I would tell my friends, 'he's not a cop!'" she laughs.

She attended parties at the YMCA with her high school friends, and her father would be sitting out front the minute the party was over. "I would never volunteer him to chaperone a high school dance. I mean, there wasn't any need," says Denise. "He'd be there anyway." In the beginning, she was annoyed when her dad showed up unannounced. Soon, she just came to expect it. She would tell people, "My dad's going to be here at 9:30, and if we're not out of here at 9:45, he's coming in."

During her senior year, she attended a cotillion with her boyfriend. Her father instructed her to call if she thought she would arrive home past her curfew. She couldn't find a phone except for one lone telephone locked in an office, which was of no use to her. Forty-five minutes later, someone yelled, "Denise, your dad is here!" She made her way outside to find her father standing there wearing a plaid jacket and a hat, and by then he had grown a distinguished-looking beard. She walked up to her father and tried to explain why she couldn't call to say she'd be late. No sooner than she could get the words out, she spotted two pay phones where dozens of coats were piled up. Her father shook his head and he laughed, "I think you should get in the car," he said. He opened the passenger side door and helped her in, then walked around to the driver's side. "I know your boyfriend doesn't know the way back, so let's see if he can keep up," he said, as he pressed the gas and took off. He was right, her boyfriend didn't know the way back. Hood pleaded for her father to slow down in order for her boyfriend to at least keep the car in his sight as he drove behind them. Her pleas fell on deaf ears. Richard knew his daughter was a good girl who didn't set out to break the rules. Besides, she maintained excellent grades in school. However, he always kept a watchful eye over her to make sure she didn't have much of an opportunity to get in trouble and felt it was important to remind her that he was the boss. After all, this was his job as a father.

That same year the school held a father daughter dance at a beautiful country club. When Richard and his daughter drove up, one of his friends who moonlighted as a valet just as he did on many occasions, greeted them, opened the car door for Hood, chatted briefly with Richard and proceeded to park their car. They went in to the dance, but Richard was having a hard time getting his tie straight. It was the type of bow tie that had to be tied just so, but Nancy hadn't been home to help her husband tie it with perfection before they left the house. He spotted another friend moonlighting as a bartender. He walked over to the bar and whispered to the friend that he was having trouble with this tie. The friend clipped off his own tie, handed it to Richard, and said, "Man, just wear a clip on, nobody will notice." Grateful, Richard shook his friend's hand, shoved his own tie in his pocket, and clipped on the tie given to him by his bartender friend. He then smiled at his daughter and they joined the other guests.

Hood quietly took in the whole experience and surmised that even though her father didn't verbalize it, this was his way of showing her that even though they were guests at the dance with her white classmates and their fathers, they have a shared history and shared experiences with the African American workers and they belong in both groups. That day, she learned the importance of acknowledging your friends, no matter the setting or circumstance. For Hood, her father didn't have to say, "Remember where you come from, and acknowledge the people that you come from." It was simply a reminder that one can and should live in these two worlds and it doesn't take any extra effort.

On a similar occasion, the father of one of Hood's classmates approached her father while they attended a school-related event at a fine restaurant. The father, a white gentleman, walked up to Richard and asked, "Sir, when are you serving dinner?"

Standing with two white fathers, he turned to the man and politely said, "You know, you're going to have to ask one of the waiters." The other fathers weren't sure how to react or what to say but Richard made nothing of it and continued to enjoy the evening. The gentleman, clearly embarrassed, also didn't know what to say. He mumbled, "Okay" and joined other guests. Perhaps it was a teachable moment for everyone who witnessed how graciously Richard handled the situation. Richard and the embarrassed father put the incident behind them and became friendly from that moment on whenever they saw one another.

When the time came to make decisions about college, Richard wanted his oldest daughter to attend a women's college. Smith, Vassar, or Wellesley topped his list of ideal schools, but he also wanted her to consider schools in Ohio like Otterbein College or Wittenberg University. Hood opposed the idea of attending college close to home. "I wanted him to have to drive all day to get to me," she admits with a laugh. "That would give my sister or my mother time to tell me that he was coming." When the Yale University recruiter came to the Columbus School for Girls he explained to Hood and her peers that the university admitted women. Yale piqued her interest, and she thought her dad would be open to the idea. The recruiter explained to her that money would not be an obstacle, that if she were admitted, the university would see to it that she had scholarships and loans to attend all four years of college. Skeptical, she wasn't quite sold on the idea and didn't understand the concept of what, today, is considered need-blind admissions, where high-performing students with demonstrated financial need are admitted to some universities regardless of their family's ability to pay tuition.

Hood didn't think it was possible to attend a prestigious university like Yale without her parents taking on a heavy financial burden, which they simply could not do. It took quite some time for the recruiter to convince her that Yale was truly an option for her. When she sat down to talk with her father about the possibility of attending Yale, he said, "Well, I'll consider it." Hood immediately thought, "I got him! I can get out of going to a woman's college if I can just get in this place." He warmed up to the idea and eventually agreed to let her go to Yale. That spring, she became the first African American graduate of Columbus School for Girls out of a class of forty-five young women. In the fall when the family drove her to New Haven, Connecticut for her freshman year of college, her father told the guard in the women's dormitory to watch out for his daughter and even pulled out her picture. The guard knew her by name and by face before he knew anyone else and he watched her as he promised her father he would.

During her matriculation at Yale, her roommate and several friends introduced her to Detroit-native, Nicholas Hood III. Reverend Hood was a graduate student at Yale pursuing a Master of Divinity degree. Quickly, they fell for one another. Richard's only expectation for his oldest daughter beyond Yale was that, armed with a four-year degree from an Ivy League university, she would find a job that would equal her potential. When she broached the subject of continuing her education he was concerned about how she was going to pay for graduate school. She explained that she would try to get a scholarship and perhaps a loan that she would ask him to co-sign for her. Her father was on board and encouraged her to go for it because as the father of two girls with unbridled potential, his dreams for them were lofty and the sky would always the limit.

She graduated from Yale in the spring of 1974 and began law school at Columbia University in New York City. She and Nicholas continued dating and she followed him to Michigan where she spent one year at the University of Michigan Law School as a visiting student. The young couple married while Hood was still in law school and soon after graduation she became a full-time Michigan resident. She took the State Bar Exam for Michigan and went to work in the city of Detroit Law Department for future United States

District Judge Anna Diggs Taylor, who became the first black woman judge appointed to the Eastern District of Michigan bench.

After working for over two years in the employment section for the city of Detroit Law Department and over two years as an assistant corporation counsel for the Water Board, with support from her parents, her husband and her politically-active, well-respected father-in-law, Reverend Dr. Nicholas Hood, Sr., she decided to run for a seat on the bench on the 36th District Court in the state of Michigan. She had just delivered the first of two healthy sons when she first ran for judgeship. She forged ahead and was elected to the 36th District Court, State of Michigan in 1982.

Not a day goes by that Hood isn't reminded of her father's life lessons. Reflecting on her father's life, Hood proudly shares that her father, Richard Page, was a good man who worked hard. He taught her that living a purpose-filled life requires lots of interests that take you beyond your circumstances so that you may truly experience what life may unfold for you. Lessons from her father were about fulfilling one's dreams—no matter what they are—and doing your absolute best with what you have.

Ronald Goldsberry, PhD

Philanthropist and Former Executive

"When my father looked at me as a family man, he responded in a visceral way. He was proud of me because he saw that I had a sense of balance in my life and he respected that."

Scores of successful philanthropists and mentors make it their life's mission to uplift, support, and nurture the next generation of business leaders and academicians. While some give of their time and financial resources because altruism runs in their family, others give because they have walked in the shoes of the young people they help educate and support. They have felt the fear of not knowing where the money for their education would come from. They have experienced sleepless nights worrying about how to succeed despite the financial odds stacked against them. Some would argue that business magnate and former chemist, Dr. Ronald Eugene Goldsberry, PhD, falls into the latter category. He is one of those exceptional leaders who believed early on that an exemplary education was within reach, but had no idea how he would pay for it.

For Goldsberry, giving back and serving as a role model have been two of his biggest priorities. In addition to chairing science-based programs and raising millions of dollars of corporate and private funds to educate African American students, he established a $100,000 scholarship at Central State University and endowed two Goldsberry scholarship funds for minorities at Michigan State University. He also established scholarship funds for minorities at Stanford University Business School.

Goldsberry graduated summa cum laude from Central State University with a Bachelor of Science degree in chemistry and went on to pursue a PhD in organic and physical chemistry from Michigan State University, and an MBA from Stanford University. He taught chemistry at the University of California at San Jose, and then enlisted in the United States Army, where he served as a captain and research chemist for the National Aeronautics and Space Administration. One of his first jobs in the private sector was as a consultant for Boston Consulting Group, where he became the firm's only African American consultant during his tenure. For the next three decades, he worked hard and positioned himself to breathe rare air as a visionary leader. He expertly climbed the ranks of several leading corporations—from director of corporate planning operations for Gulf Oil Corporation to Ford Motor Company's global vice president for customer service, where he managed 14,000 employees and oversaw Ford's markets in Asia, Eastern Europe and South America.

Born in 1942 and raised in working-class Wilmington, Delaware to Dr. Clifford Isaacs and Constance Jones Wright, Goldsberry is no stranger to success, yet what he wanted most was to have a relationship with his father. This father-son relationship, however, would not come until later in life and would prove for Goldsberry to be worth the wait. Dr. Clifford Isaacs was born in Savannah, Georgia in 1923 and, as a young boy, moved to Wilmington, Delaware with his uncle. Dr. Isaacs was an only child growing up in a working class black neighborhood in Wilmington, where his uncle and aunt owned a convenience store. He attended Howard High School, where he met Constance Jones Wright, a young lady one year his junior. Constance became pregnant with Dr. Isaacs's child during her senior year of high school and gave birth to Ronald Eugene on September 12, 1942. The young couple did not stay together and Dr. Isaacs did not raise his only son. He left Wilmington, enlisted in the United States Army. After being honorably discharged, he moved to Detroit to live with his father and stepmother. In Detroit, he continued his education and became a pharmacist and later a doctor.

Dr. Isaacs visited Wilmington from time to spend time with his son and other family members. When Goldsberry was young, his mother got married and his stepfather, John Goldsberry, began to take issue with Dr. Isaacs's infrequent visits and the conditions under which he saw the young boy. Soon Dr. Isaacs's visits became less frequent and not as memorable for the boy. When Goldsberry got a little older his aunt made sure that when his dad was in town, they got the chance to spend quality time together. Goldsberry maintained communication with his father over the years by phone and by mail, but years passed between visits.

Goldsberry was raised in an extremely religious environment and the family belonged to Mt. Calvary Church of God in Christ, a fundamentalist, storefront church in Wilmington. Goldsberry had to go to church almost every day and for most of the day each Sunday. Members of the congregation couldn't play sports or dance. Goldsberry rebelled and even went through an agnostic phase that eventually passed. One of his greatest influences was the pastor of the church, Bishop Blackshear, or "Bishop," as his congregation affectionately called him. "Nobody is perfect, but I thought he walked on water. I was like one of his sons, and I was very close to his kids whom I grew up with," Ron says. "He literally built his own churches from the ground up, and as a little boy, I couldn't wait to be his assistant so I could go and get the bricks and help him. I loved him like a father, particularly because I missed my own father."

Although Goldsberry felt a void from his father's absence, he felt that one day the two would reunite. Until then, his education became a primary focal point, and he poured his heart and soul into his studies. Upon graduating in the top five of his high school class in 1960, he decided to attend Central State University in Ohio, one of the nation's historically black colleges and universities. He likened traveling the 520 miles from Delaware to Ohio to traveling to the other side of the world. It was a time in his life when he felt young and fearless and desperately wanted to gain a sense of independence. He admits, however, that after he got to campus, he was scared and called his mother every day begging to come home. But she refused to let him give up. By this time, his stepfather had passed away from Leukemia and his mother didn't have money for college tuition and expenses. Goldsberry came up with a plan, sought financial assistance, applied for scholarships, and worked his way through school.

During his senior year, one of his roommates, whose father was also a doctor, learned of Goldsberry's upbringing in Wilmington and his father's absence. He urged Goldsberry to go see his dad, who lived in Detroit. "My roommate always said, 'Ron, we have to find a way for you to see your dad. We can go to Detroit to party and hang out and it will give you an opportunity for you to see him.' We were big time partying Ques, so there was probably going to be some Que party in Detroit," Ron laughs, referring to Omega Psi Phi, the fraternity he pledged as a college sophomore.

Goldsberry agreed that traveling to Detroit, where his father was the chief surgeon at Mt. Clemens Hospital, was a good idea. He called his dad, told him of his plans to be in town, and expressed his desire to see him. It was the first time in his young adult life that he took a proactive step to establish more of a relationship with his dad. In Goldsberry's eyes, his father was this larger-than-life figure whom he admired from afar. "My dad managed to transition from being poor, not having his mom and dad raise him, to overcoming these challenges and becoming a doctor," Ron reflects. "As far as I was concerned, if he was a doctor, he was without question one of the top leaders in the community."

While in college, Goldsberry considered becoming a doctor himself. He even interned in the obstetrics and gynecology department of a hospital where he witnessed his first caesarian section. After what he felt was a harrowing experience he thought, "Oh my goodness, I don't know if I can take this." Once Goldsberry began to spend time with his father, he realized his dad's entire life was devoted to his medical practice, and he did not have a healthy work-life balance. As their relationship developed, father and son discussed the fact that one of Goldsberry's reasons for initially being interested in medicine was to meet his dad's expectations, although admittedly, he had no idea what those expectations were. Goldsberry had conjured up expectations in his own mind and rationalized that the reason his dad did not have a relationship with him was because he was not good enough.

When he looked at his dad's life, he didn't know whether he wanted to be like him or if his dad served as a motivator for him to reach even greater heights, just to prove to himself that he was worthy of his father's love and respect. "Why isn't he accepting me in his life?" Ron would ask himself. It occurred to him over the years that some men at all stages of life often carry hurt from disappointment and unfulfilled expectations and this is a conversation that fathers and sons need to have with each other and with other men in their lives.

Though he was an excellent, focused student with great potential to succeed in anything he decided to pursue, Goldsberry struggled with feeling inadequate and felt his dad had set the bar extremely high. Goldsberry's sole purpose became to "over succeed" so he could get to that bar. It wasn't until he could say to himself, "Okay, I'm at a pretty high bar now that's at least as good as or maybe better than the bar I think my dad set." And it was sort of a magical moment for the extraordinary, accomplished man who went on to earn his PhD and become a trailblazing African American corporate executive.

Goldsberry remembers talking with his dad about the medical field and Dr. Isaacs told him in no uncertain terms that if he had to choose a career for him, it would not be a physician. This came as a shock to Goldsberry because although it really wasn't in his heart to be a physician, medicine was a career path he was strongly considering. "That was around the time of serious issues concerning legislation and malpractice insurance when malpractice insurance might cost physicians' more than three to six months of their salary," Ron explained. "Before that time, being a physician was a relatively lucrative career, but this was at that tipping point when things started to change for doctors."

Reflecting on this pivotal moment, Goldsberry thought his father had the foresight that the medical profession was not going to be in the future what it had once been. This was great advice from an economic standpoint, but he read into it even beyond the financial concerns. He understood that a career decision of this magnitude should be something you're doing because you're passionate about it, not strictly for the money. Goldsberry has always felt that some professions have to do with a life calling and others are simply about financial gain. He has always been able to always separate the two.

As Goldsberry's career began an upward trajectory, he made it a point to get to Detroit to see his father whenever he could. During a short period, he worked for Gulf Oil Corporation in Houston, Texas. He traveled to the Midwest to see his dad, this time bringing his wife and two children, whom Dr. Isaacs had never met. When Dr. Isaacs saw his grandchildren, Ryan and Renee, there was a glimmer in his eye. He later divulged to his son that seeing him with a wife and children—a life that he never enjoyed for himself—mattered far more than his son's education or his professional accolades. When Goldsberry reflects on how his father reacted to meeting his family, his heart swells with pride because pleasing his father mattered a great deal to him. "I just think he was proud of me from that standpoint," admits Ron. "Not that he wanted that for himself because he was very successful, but he saw that I had balance in my life and I think he respected that."

In the early 1980s, Goldsberry relocated to the Detroit area to take a high-profile position with Parker Chemical Company and received a great deal of publicity when the appointment was announced. "So here's this guy that comes to Detroit, a guy that's trying to impress his dad," he says with a laugh. "Hey dad, let's have dinner!" the successful executive said to his dad once he and his family had finally settled into their new home. Once again, Goldsberry kept the relationship alive, and his father was always receptive and ready to meet him half way. During this time, father and son got to know each other very well.

Goldsberry discovered that his father loved music. He loved to dance, and yet he had this other side that was very private and closed. He found it somewhat challenging to bring out some of the more personal parts of his father's life. Goldsberry discovered that the best way to get in touch with his father was through Carol, Dr. Isaacs chief nurse who later became his executive assistant and confidante. She gave Goldsberry insight into how Dr. Isaacs structured his work and personal life. She would graciously help Goldsberry find the best ways to stay connected with his dad. "Dr. Isaacs doesn't really say what's on his mind," Carol would tell him. "I'll kill you if you ever tell him this, but he's got all of these press clippings of you." He couldn't believe that his father saved the press coverage of his appointment to his new position with Parker Chemical Company.

Dr. Isaacs never talked about whether or not he was proud of his son's success, but it stands to reason that he was. Carol would tell the young executive the times that were open on his father's schedule and suggest when he should arrive at the doctor's house to meet him. She also let him in on the secret that his dad was a huge sports fan who loved the Detroit sports teams. Dr. Isaacs had season tickets to the Detroit Pistons and Detroit Tigers games. Goldsberry would join his father and some of his father's colleagues for the games. Father and son cherished the time together, and Goldsberry continued to go to the games after his dad died. He took over the season tickets as sort of a lasting tribute to his dad.

While he experienced and lived with the profound disappointment of not growing up with and being shaped by his father during his formidable years, having a relationship with his dad as an adult became extremely important. He always felt that he didn't want his children to have the same type of childhood he had, where he wondered what his father would say or how he would react to his many academic achievements. Would his dad have been there on the front row when he graduated summa cum laude from college? Would he have shown up for his gospel choir performances when he was a teenager? Would his father have packed up the car filled with his belongings and driven him to college?

Goldsberry would never know, but what he learned is that so many people take their parents for granted. Because of the relationship gaps with his father, he never takes his own children for granted, nor does he allow them to take him for granted. He talks to his children about the how important their relationship is and takes time to talk to other kids as well. "It's one of these things that unless you've experienced it, it's hard to understand what you've missed," Ron admits. He also admits that as a parent, he has in some ways, tried to overcompensate for not having his dad in his life. "I remember when I used to bring my kids to my dad's place and he'd say 'Wow, you're spoiling those kids,'" says Ron. "I honestly think that was more of a generational thing. Parents and people that grew up in my dad's generation always thought that we were too generous to our kids."

Goldsberry spent a lot of time with his dad near the end of his life. Even when Dr. Isaacs became ill and almost too weak to stand, he wanted to be in the operating room to perform surgery but his partners had to tell him no, that it was a bad idea both physically and legally. Allowing him to be in the operating room to observe was a fair compromise, and Dr. Isaacs was satisfied just being there. That's the kind of passion the dedicated physician had for his profession.

In 1988, Dr. Isaacs became gravely ill. Goldsberry went to the hospital every day to spend time with him. His dad would say, "You're a busy person, and I'm going to be okay so you don't have to stay here with me."

To this, Goldsberry would reply, "You're not in control now. I'm in control." For him, it was important to be there by his father's side. This was probably his fondest memory because he got what he always wanted—time just to be with his dad.

Dr. Isaacs never explained why he wasn't there as Goldsberry was growing up and never said, "I'm sorry." Much to Goldsberry's chagrin, he and his father never had *that* conversation. He did, however, have the conversation with his mom later in his life as an adult. "I think my mom felt obligated to let me know why things happened the way they did and for me to understand that it wasn't my dad's decision not to be there for me," says Ron. "Essentially she was saying, 'Don't blame your father.'" Despite the fact that it took years for them to establish a relationship, Goldsberry views his father, Dr. Clifford Isaacs, as the most dedicated, committed, passionate physician that he has or will ever know and the loving relationship he developed with his dad over time made him appreciate and understand the true importance of fatherhood from both a father and a son's perspective.

Harold Ford, Jr.

Former United States Congressman

"If everybody had a father like I had growing up, the world would be a safer and far more humane place."

No matter what side of the political aisle one stands on, it's hard to deny that success breeds success, particularly in the Ford family. From 1997 to 2007, Harold Eugene Ford, Jr. walked in his father's political footsteps serving Tennessee's 9th District in the United States Congress. Charismatic and confident like his father; Ford was once described by former President, Bill Clinton, as "the walking, living embodiment of where America ought to go in the twenty-first century."

Ford's father, Harold Sr., became the first African American to represent Tennessee in Congress, an office he held for more than two decades. He was the first, and is the only African American Democrat to unseat an incumbent Republican congressman in a predominantly white district. When he left the House of Representatives, his son won the seat making them the only African Americans elected to federal office from Tennessee in the modern era.

In 2006 the younger Ford lost his bid for U.S. Senate by a narrow margin. He was asked to chair the Democratic Leadership Council in 2007 and later that year joined Fox News as an analyst where he stayed for a year before leaving for a similar role at NBC and MSNBC. Also in 2007, Ford joined Merrill Lynch as a vice-chairman and accepted an assignment to teach in the political science department at Vanderbilt University. Today, Ford is a managing director at Morgan Stanley and a professor of public policy at New York University's Wagner School of Public Service.

The eighth of fifteen children born to Newton Jackson Ford and Vera Ford, the elder Harold came into the world in the spring of 1945. Harold Sr.'s father was the founder and owner of a successful funeral home in South Memphis. He was also a leader in the community and a lifetime member of the NAACP. Although Newton, affectionately known by everyone as NJ, lost a bid for the Tennessee state legislature in 1965, he was elected as a delegate to the Tennessee Constitutional Convention in 1977. He helped fund children's education and sports programs and was an active supporter of the Boy Scouts of America. Newton's role as a community and business leader has a tremendous impact on Harold Sr. and his brothers.

Harold Sr. graduated from Geeter High School in 1963. All of the Ford children went to Tennessee State University to pursue their undergraduate degrees. Because all of his siblings attended TSU, the elder Harold came to campus with a bit of a legacy. He became very active on campus and successfully ran for and won the position of class president. He earned his Bachelor's degree from Tennessee State University in Nashville in 1967 and did graduate work there for one year. During their time on campus, Harold Sr. and his siblings were well known and well respected. Years later, a freshmen dorm was erected in honor of Harold Sr. and his older brother, John, who served as a member of the Tennessee State Senate.

The elder Harold married Dorothy Jean Bowles in 1969. Dorothy was also born and raised in Memphis. Harold Sr. and Dorothy welcomed their first child, Harold Jr. into the world May 11, 1970. Their second child, Jake, was born in 1972, and their third child, Isaac, was born in 1975. That same year, Harold Sr. received a Mortuary Science degree from John A. Gupton College of Nashville in 1969. He later earned his MBA from Howard University 1982.

In 1970 Harold Sr. ran a successful campaign and was elected to the Tennessee House of Representatives, becoming one of its youngest members and one of only a few African Americans to have served in the Tennessee General Assembly to that point in the 20th century. Then, on November 4, 1974, he won his congressional seat and two of his brothers, John and Emmitt, won their respective races for State Senate and State House. It was the first time in American history that three brothers had been on the same ballot on the same day and all won.

Harold Sr.'s enormous role in Tennessee politics had a lasting impact on his oldest son. As a member of one of Tennessee's most influential and prominent political families, Ford was always interested in politics. His father took him along to many of his meetings and speaking engagements. The younger Ford recalls giving his first political speech at age four in the form of a political radio ad for his dad. These experiences not only shaped his childhood, but also they also influenced his desire to go into politics and strengthened the relationship he has with his dad to this very day.

As a young boy who spent years watching his father navigate national and local politics, Ford learned that his dad handles challenges with courage and valor. "As a political leader, my father never shied away from tough times," referring to his father's role on the select committee to investigate the death, among others, of Martin Luther King, Jr. and his fight to clear his name in the 1987 indictment on bank fraud charges. "Not that he sought fights, acrimony, or controversy, but when challenges came his way he would take them head on." Ford also feels that his father, whom he describes as full of energy and outgoing, is the life of any room he is in. He appreciated watching how his dad made friends with everyone, whether they agreed with his politics or not.

His father was elected to Congress when Ford was four, and the family moved to Washington, DC when he was nine. Even after moving to Washington, the family kept very close ties to Memphis, where the Ford boys spent their summers. Today, Ford remains close to many members of his extended family. His late grandmother and Ford family matriarch, Vera, made Sunday dinner at her home, the meeting place for the family until her death in 1993. "I learned family lessons and history at those dinners that will stick with me forever," Ford says fondly.

Like many congressmen and women, Harold Sr. was not always present as his boys were growing up, but Ford says his dad "couldn't have been more supportive." He continued, "My mom sat on the edge of her seat at soccer, football and basketball games. She helped with the homework and attended most school meetings. And she was the disciplinarian," Harold says. "My mother handled all the belts and switch responsibilities. She believed in serious physical discipline. My dad never engaged in the belts and all of that, but we were scared of my dad. When he came home and told us to do something, we jumped into action."

Harold Sr. and Dorothy exposed their sons to the idea of faith and spirituality, and the important role both must play in their lives. In Memphis, the Ford family attended Mt. Moriah-East Baptist Church where all of the boys were baptized. In DC, the family attended New Bethel Baptist Church, pastored by Walter Fauntroy, one of Harold Sr.'s colleagues in Congress. The family occasionally attended Metropolitan Church, pastored by their neighbor and good friend, Dr. Ivan Hicks. In addition, Ford went to church service twice a week at school. As much as his parents influenced him to walk a spiritual path, Ford's middle and high school experience at St. Albans also had a powerful influence in his life.

Nicknamed the chairman by Ford's childhood friends, Harold Sr. was close to many of his sons' friends. "All of our buddies loved my dad and kind of feared him too," says Harold. But many of Ford's friends had parents in politics or in business in DC so all of the parents were friends and often did things together professionally.

When it was time for Ford to begin looking at colleges, his father encouraged him to make his own decision. He knew with certainty that although his father and many of his family members went to college in their native Tennessee, he didn't have much interest in following that same path. To be sure, he went on a college visit to Vanderbilt University in Nashville where administrators and students alike asked him if he was the son of Congressman Ford. While he has always loved being his father's son, he was in search of a little independence and wanted the chance to be his own man. He decided to go to the University of Pennsylvania, and in 1988 his father and mother drove him to campus and helped him move into his dorm room. Before leaving, Harold Sr. and Dorothy hung a very large University of Pennsylvania flag on the wall. Underneath the lettering was the number "1992." His father explained why they hung it. "We want you to see '1992' every morning when you wake up, because after that, we're not paying one dime for you to go to college. You need to understand that."

While in college, Ford gave some thought to practicing law and even thought briefly that he might try his hand at journalism. A gifted writer, Ford cofounded Penn's black student newspaper, *The Vision,* and also wrote a twice-monthly column for the school's daily paper, *The Daily Pennsylvanian*. During this time, he reflected on lessons from his father of developing a strong work ethic and thought about how to apply these lessons to his own life. His dad often shared stories about the jobs he worked when he was seven and eight years old and how he worked his way through college waiting tables. These lessons made Ford appreciate how incredibly ambitious his dad has always been. They also made him realize how blessed he is to have parents who paid for him to go to college, but also taught him the value of developing a sense of independence and ownership over his own life. His dad encouraged him to work his way through college to help pay for some of the things he wanted to do and he got his father's message of independence loud and clear, graduating with a degree in American history right on time.

At graduation, Ford received the Spoon Award, symbolic of first honors among senior men at the University of Pennsylvania. He could sense how elated his father was because "my dad gets to moving real fast when he's excited about something," Harold says, laughing. His father teared up when he received the award, and he could see in his father's eyes, how incredibly proud he was. When Ford graduated with honors from the University of Michigan Law School in 1996 and later, when he delivered the keynote address at the 2000 Democratic National Convention in Los Angeles, he saw that same look of pride in his dad's eyes.

After graduating from college, Ford went back and forth to Memphis to support his father during the trials following the indictment on bank fraud charges that alleged Harold Sr. had used business loans for his personal needs. Harold Sr. denied and fought the charges claiming the prosecution was politically motivated. He remained in Congress but was forced to give up his leadership posts. During this difficult period, Ford and his father grew closer. In Ford's book, *More Davids Than Goliaths: A Political Education*, he writes in great detail about the emotional rollercoaster he experienced when his father was indicted and went through not one, but two criminal trials. The first ended in a mistrial. In the second, a jury of eleven whites and one African American acquitted him of all charges. It was a real growing up period for Ford in many ways, particularly during his father's second trial. The young Ford had recently graduated from college and was working for the late Ron Brown, the United States Secretary of Commerce, and the first African American to hold this position. After working for Secretary Brown for only five weeks, Ford went to Memphis with his dad and was in the courtroom by his side every day. He wore many hats during the trial—everything from getting his dad coffee to acting as one of his advisors. This became a real turning point in their relationship. "I think about moments we've had together and Good Friday 1993—the day my dad's innocence was validated by the jury—will always stand out as among the best in our relationship," Harold says.

As close as father and son are, when Ford decided to run for Congress, he had to convince his father that he was fit to serve the people as congressman. Harold Sr. was his son's toughest, most demanding, and most rigorous critic. Even after the young congressman won the election and had been sworn into office, his father remained his "*real* opponent and the standard I was expected to uphold." Harold says. As a newly elected congressman, he felt a lot of pressure because he knew he had big shoes to fill. People knew of his father's legacy and loved him. His father ran a phenomenal constituent service operation, and Ford knew he had to live up to that more than anything else.

The night Ford was elected to Congress, he and his father shared another indelible moment right before he took the stage to thank supporters. He asked his father if he had any advice he could share as he began his journey into politics. Ford was specifically referring to advice about what he should say in front of his crowd of constituents and supporters that evening, but what his dad shared will always stay with him. "Number one, always put the people first; and number two, always put the people first," Harold Sr. told his son.

This moment reminded Ford in so many ways of his first campaign speech that his dad heard. But this time, Ford was speaking before 5,000 people at his father's annual prayer breakfast at the Peabody Hotel in Memphis. The crowd was larger than normal because it was Ford's introduction to the broader community, and it was a test of his readiness and composure, both of which had been questioned by the local press and critics. Although Harold Sr. had heard his son speak in smaller settings, this was the first time he heard him speak before a large group.

Ford's speech went extremely well. The crowd approved, and equally important, so did Harold Sr. "Before today," Harold Sr. said to the audience after his son's speech," I was going to vote for Harold Jr. After hearing him today, I plan to work and follow him throughout this campaign, and I'm asking all of you to do the same," he said. His father's very public outpouring of support before so many important people overwhelmed the newly elected congressman and is something he will never forget.

Just as Ford has always been able to sense when his father is pleased, he knows in no uncertain terms when he is disappointed. When his dad didn't like something or didn't agree with something he did, he made his displeasure very clear. During Ford's ten years in Congress, many of his opponents and critics knew of the close relationship he shared with his father. His dad never called him to express favor for an issue or disappointment in a vote. Harold Sr. would, however, call to give his son advice on constituent service, which always echoed his election night admonition—*Always put the people first.* In fact, the only thing that drew the elder Ford's ire was when he heard of Ford Jr. or his staff being late returning constituent calls or requests. It didn't happen often but when it did, Harold remembers. "My dad tolerated lots but had no tolerance for *not* responding to the people," Harold recalls. Fortunately those calls were rare from father to son. "My dad's love and respect for politics at its core is rooted in service, especially to the last and the least. That is the most enduring lesson my dad has taught me about politics," Harold says.

When doing constituent service work, he always remembered his dad's persistence and perseverance. His father was never the kind of person to call and beat people up. Rather, he would kill people with kindness, and would identify the exact problem, then proceed to do everything in his power to fix it. "I can hear his voice in my head all the time saying, 'We gotta fix this,'" Harold said. "No matter what's going on you always want to help people. Once you get into it, it's hard to shake it. This is one of the most important lessons I learned from my father."

Since leaving office, he and his father continue to talk regularly about politics, policy and sports. "We talk every morning and often a few more times a day," Harold says. "My dad gets a kick out of my work in the private sector now. He often shares his candid views about Wall Street during our conversations. I think he likes telling his buddies, 'My son explained this to me' or 'Did you see him on *Morning Joe* or *Meet The Press* talking about this?'"

In 2008, Ford married Emily Threlkeld. They do not have any children yet, but when they do he plans to be an active and engaged father. "I want to be around a lot when I have kids, no doubt about that," Harold says. "I love my Dad, he's my best friend."

Robin Roberts (right) with her father, Colonel Lawrence Edward Roberts

Reverend Nicholas Hood III (left) with his father, Reverend Dr. Nicholas Hood Sr.

Rosalind Brewer's father, George Gates

Rosalind Brewer, The first African American female President and CEO of Sam's Club, a division of Wal-Mart Stores, Inc.

Russell Simmons, Cultural Icon and Master Entrepreneur

Ilyasah Shabazz in the arms of her father, Malcolm X

Andrew Young, Jr. (back row, right), celebrates with members of his family election night November 1972 when he became the first African American from the deep South since Reconstruction elected to Congress from the 5th District of Georgia. His father, Andrew Young, Sr. is pictured front row, right.

Former Congressman, Harold Ford, Jr.

Denise Page Hood, United States District Court Judge

*Denise Page Hood's parents, Nancy and Richard Page at
Nancy's high school prom*

Dr. Ronald Goldsberry, PhD

Ron Goldsberry's father, Dr. Clifford Isaacs with two of his grandchildren

Dennis Archer (center) with his sons and grandsons

Kim Harris Jones being escorted down the aisle by her tearful father, Fred "Chink" Harris

Stefan Holt (left), with his father, Lester Holt, on set at NBC 5 Chicago Studios

Congresswoman Yvette D. Clarke (left) with her father, Leslie Lloyd Clarke, Sr.

Allan Houston (left), with his father and college coach, Wade Houston

Dr. Thurman E. Hunt (right), with his father, Delbert Wesley Hunt, Sr.

Major General Marcia M. Anderson's father, Rudolph Mahan, who served in the United States Air Force during the Korean War

Major General Marcia M. Anderson, the first African American woman awarded a second star as a general in the United States Army

Tracy Maitland, Wall Street Investment Manager

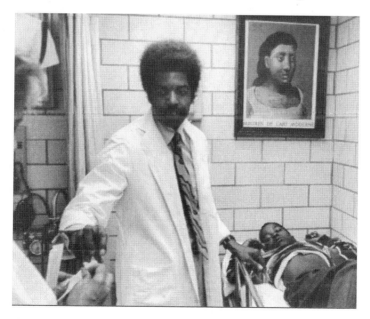

Dr. Leo C. Maitland, father of Tracy Maitland

Juana Wooldridge (right), with her father, David Wooldridge, Jr.

John Rogers, Jr. (left), with his father, The Honorable John Rogers, Sr.

Dr. Velma Scantlebury (left), with her father, Delacey Scantlebury

Dennis W. Archer

Former Mayor of Detroit and Michigan Supreme Court Justice

"Even though my dad did not have the financial wherewithal, he gave me the fundamentals that allowed me to be who I am."

The Honorable Dennis W. Archer sometimes sees his father in a dream. He doesn't know what triggers the dream, but he wakes up with a profound sense that Ernest Archer is proud of all that his only son has achieved in this lifetime. Although Dennis Archer has served as a public school teacher, attorney, and Michigan State Supreme Court Justice, he perhaps is best known as the 67th mayor of Detroit and the first African American to become president of the American Bar Association. The two-term mayor whose community development efforts in Detroit brought him national acclaim has long been admired and respected for leading with class and honor, and he is held in high regard as a man never afraid to tell the truth. Today, Archer serves as chairman and CEO of Dennis W. Archer PLLC and as chairman emeritus of the Detroit-based law firm, Dickinson Wright.

Archer felt the sting of poverty as a child growing up in Cassopolis, Michigan—a village of less than two square miles with a population of 1,500. Living below the poverty line, however, is not what stuck with him. It was the love he received from his father and mother—love that eclipsed hungry nights and taught him that he possessed the resilience and the drive to accomplish things that seemed far beyond his reach. While the early part of his life may be seen as a lesson in survival, it is equally a lesson in love—the love of a son and his father who cherished time together and embraced the fundamental values of respect and integrity.

Archer speaks with intensity and purpose about the challenges he faced during his formidable years and the bond he shared with his father, Ernest. Though Ernest was permanently disabled by the loss of an arm in an automobile accident before Dennis was born, he never let his physical challenges make him feel inferior or prevent him from being a good husband and father.

Archer's mother, Frances Marie Carroll Archer, was a kind-hearted, spiritual woman from Tazewell, Virginia. She was a guiding light in Archer's life making sure he attended Sunday school followed by church service on Sundays and again on Wednesdays. Frances taught her only son patience. She taught him compassion. She taught him to work mightily and love unconditionally. Frances taught her son that nothing worth having is easy and that the conditions one inherits in life should in no way define them.

Ernest James Archer was the rock of the family. He taught the future mayor that the content of his character and the power of his convictions were just as important as the lessons he learned in school. In an era when men were viewed—and in turn viewed themselves—primarily as breadwinners and providers, Archer's father taught him to love and respect himself and others—values that show up in his life to this very day.

Archer was born on a cold, blustery Thursday afternoon in January 1942. The weeks preceding his birth were met with great anxiety by his parents. Money was always tight, and there were no hospitals in Cassopolis, which meant they would have to travel to Niles, Michigan or South Bend, Indiana for Frances to deliver their first and only child. The young couple agreed that it would be better for the baby to be born in Detroit, 187 miles northeast of Cassopolis, where Frances would have the support of her family and access to reliable medical care. Once their son arrived, Frances and Ernest decided it was in the family's best interest for mother and baby to stay in Detroit at least for a while. That while turned into five years.

"My grandmother's house was in what was referred to as Black Bottom, so as a very young boy, I saw black folks and there were black businesses," says Dennis. To this day, positive images of entrepreneurs in Black Bottom are a great source of pride for Archer. When he turned five, his parents decided it was time for the family to be together in Cassopolis. He recalls that leaving Detroit, meeting his father for the first time and living in an unfamiliar place was unsettling at first. More unsettling perhaps was the idea of leaving a modest but comfortable home and lifestyle in the city to move to a rural area that lacked the creature comforts he was used to. Archer recalls that he hated taking baths in his grandmother's bathtub in Detroit, but when he and his mother settled into life with his father in Cassopolis he looked back on and appreciated those warm baths on colds nights, especially when he found himself bathing every Saturday night in a metal tub until he graduated from high school. He would sometimes visit his grandmother in Detroit or his uncle in Chicago where he could take a bath or a shower indoors and enjoy well-balanced meals. Enjoying all of these amenities was bittersweet because he had to go back home where the struggles continued.

The Archer family home in Cassopolis had an outhouse, a kerosene stove, and water that Frances used to wash dishes and bathe. There was a pump outside of the house and when the pump dried up, Archer would go to the neighboring business to run water from the outdoor faucet. He would fill a bucket with water, bring it back to the house, and put newspaper on top of the bucket to prevent dust from getting in the water. Archer can recall dinners when his mother would serve only biscuits and sometimes without butter or honey. Inevitably they would run out of money. And as he grew older, he had one pair of shoes that he played in and went to school and church in. He didn't have many clothes, but his clothes were clean, and to him that was most important.

Growing up, Archer could readily see that there were not a lot of opportunities in Cassopolis, Michigan, particularly for people of color. Racism—sometimes subtle, though usually overt—permeated many facets of life in this small town made up of a one block long main street with two banks, two grocery stores, two pharmacies, one bakery, a bar and a cabstand. To his recollection not one person of color owned a business or worked during the light of day on Main Street. In fact, African Americans were not seen much at all on Main Street particularly during business hours, although behind the scenes they stocked groceries, swept floors, and tended to the needs of the business owners for very little pay.

Although most families didn't have telephones, when the school had snow days, they would find a way to go to a classmate's house to play bid whist. As he got older, Archer never had friends over. Unlike his peers whose homes had bathrooms, he was ashamed that they did not have indoor plumbing, and he refused to subject his friends to using the bathroom outside. While these experiences were humbling and he sometimes felt ashamed, he understood that hard times wouldn't last always, and he did everything he could to help his family.

One day while driving a car belonging to his employer, Ernest pointed out a marker along M-60 and explained to his curious son that the marker indicated a stop on the Underground Railroad. Archer asked his father, "Dad, how did they build a railroad underground?" His father smiled and explained what he meant by Underground Railroad. Archer was astonished to learn that the Underground Railroad was a vast, organized system and network of people who helped fugitive slaves escape to the North and Canada toward the end of the 18th century. This example of their quality time together stuck with Archer and made him appreciate the many lessons he learned from his beloved father.

The elder Archer had a prosthesis that never quite fit properly; therefore, he didn't bother to wear it. "My father could do anything anybody else did," Dennis says. "His disability never deterred him." Archer remembers wrestling with his dad. "He would take that little nub of his left arm and wear me out." His father also taught him how to work with electricity and to this day, Archer can fix any lamp and most anything in need of repair.

One summer Archer's father taught him how to grow a garden. The elder Archer not only taught him to grow fruits and vegetables, but also he spent a great deal of time talking with his son every chance he got. They talked about taking care of a garden. They talked about family. They talked about life and the world they lived in. It was in this soil, you see, that seeds far more important than those yielding fruits and vegetables were planted. The seeds his father planted were ones that provided Archer with a lifetime of lessons. Listening to Archer reflect on his days working in the garden, one can almost picture them side by side with their hands steeped in the rich Cassopolis soil. "The fruits and vegetables my family did not eat, I occasionally sold to neighbors," he says. "I would walk down the road selling red raspberries, corn, and the like." Archer never shied away from greeting people he knew as well as those unfamiliar to him as he sold the homegrown produce. Though it was hard work, he became comfortable presenting himself and talking with adults. He mastered the art of closing the deal. Archer took on this role with pride for he knew that ultimately it helped his family and gave him confidence to go on to do great things in his lifetime.

Everyone in Cassopolis knew when report cards came out whether they had children or not. "Dennis, come over here and let me see that report card!" a neighbor would yell. If he got good grades the neighbors would pat him on the head and give him a piece of candy. If he didn't get the kinds of grades he had the potential of earning, they were quick to express their disappointment: "You ought to be shamed of yourself. You need to do better." Even before he moved to Cassopolis, every elder in Archer's life—his grandmother, aunts, uncles or family friends—focused on making sure he and all children worked hard to get good grades.

Archer was brought up with the mindset that if you wanted something and didn't have any money, you worked and saved for it. He was proud to show his father that he was willing to work in order to help the family and so that he didn't have to ask for anything. His first job was a caddy at a golf course when he was just eight years old. Following his job as a caddy, Archer set pins in a bowling alley. In high school he rose before dawn to walk over a mile to downtown Cassopolis to work at the town bakery. Once he arrived at the bakery, he swept and mopped the floors, and then walked back home to get ready for school. While working at the bakery, the father of one of his classmates who owned an interior decorating business heard stories of Archer waking before sunrise to work and felt sorry for him. The father talked with Archer and felt that if he was energetic enough to do more at five o'clock in the morning than some people do in an entire day, he could learn the art of soldering. He hired Archer to solder and polish metal.

Archer worked hard but also enjoyed many of the things living in Cassopolis afforded him like playing in the marching band and being on the high school golf team and the basketball team. One year with Archer coming off the bench, his high school basketball team had a glorious season remaining undefeated until Kalamazoo Christian beat them in the regional finals. Learning the value of hard work and teamwork helped lay the foundation for Archer's adult life and because of his upbringing in Cassopolis and his father's guidance, it would never occur to him to rob someone, steal, or do something wrong. Bringing harm to others was never an option.

This legacy of valuing education began in Detroit's Black Bottom neighborhood where he first saw positive examples of people of color going to school, raising strong families, and running businesses. Despite the fact that he grew up in poverty, his mother who earned a high school diploma, and his father, who had only a third grade education, made it clear to him that he was going to college. They couldn't tell him where to go or what to major in because neither Ernest nor Frances had ever set foot on a college campus. "My parents taught me that if I wanted to make something out of my life, I must get a good education," Archer says. "An education is something no one can ever take away from you, and despite all that our society has in terms of materials things, we seem not to possess the values I think are important, that help so many people like me appreciate and respect others," Dennis explains.

Archer loved his parents and his hometown, but he knew that ultimately a life for him existed beyond the two-mile radius of Cassopolis. In 1959, with nothing to lose and the whole world to gain, he packed up his ambitions, the lessons learned from his father and moved to Detroit to live with his grandmother. In Detroit he took a job as a painter for a real estate company. He did what he had to do but knew that painting was a short-term means to an end. Soon Archer went to work for his uncle, a real estate salesman, and took an additional job as a stock boy at a neighborhood drugstore. By this time Archer had accomplished one of many goals: He was officially enrolled as a freshman at Wayne State University. His uncle's wife told him of an opportunity for college students to work in the evenings in the medical records department of Henry Ford Hospital where she worked as an elevator operator. Archer applied for and landed the job, becoming the first black person to work in the medical records department at Henry Ford Hospital.

After studying at Wayne State University, he transferred to the Detroit Institute of Arts. He was fulfilling his course requirements to graduate when it dawned on him that he couldn't think of anything to do with a degree in arts and sciences. After giving it a great deal of thought and researching what he thought would be an interesting career, he decided to become a teacher and transferred to Western Michigan University where he graduated with a Bachelor of Arts degree in special education. Archer worked his way through college, managing to pay most of his tuition and expenses for his books. When he walked across the stage to receive his college diploma in 1963, he owed the university only $1,500.

After graduation Archer began teaching special education students, and he enjoyed the experience immensely. He enjoyed teaching, but there was something truly special to him about working with young people. The school principal observed Archer's aptitude for teaching special education students and saw great potential in him. She suggested that he go to graduate school to earn a Master's degree with the goal of becoming a principal. He decided to pursue this career track, but after enrolling in two classes in a University of Michigan extension program, he discovered that he would be learning from the same two textbooks that he used in undergraduate classes at Western Michigan University. He couldn't imagine what he was going to learn out of those same textbooks and began to feel as though pursuing an advanced degree in education wasn't in his best interest.

While Archer stood at this crossroads, a lovely teacher encouraged him to go to law school. He complained to her that he didn't know anything about law. She listened to his incessant whining and patiently suggested on several more occasions that he strongly consider earning a law degree. This went on for a while until he agreed to take the LSAT exam. His score on the exam suggested that if he went to law school he could probably earn his law degree and become a lawyer. He decided to go for it. He taught during the day and went to law school at night at Detroit

College of Law. The lovely teacher was right by his side encouraging and supporting him along the way. By his account, law school was a solid accomplishment, but perhaps the wisest decision Archer could have made was to ask for the teacher, Trudy DunCombe's hand in marriage. On June 17, 1967 the two were married at Blessed Sacrament Cathedral in Detroit. Trudy also went on to become a successful lawyer and later served as a judge in the 36th District Court for seventeen years.

Throughout his career, Archer has been reminded of the lessons his father taught him. While he doesn't necessarily hear his father's voice, he remembers his hands in the soil of their garden. He remembers the sense of pride his father expressed when he brought home good grades. He remembers his dad serving as an excellent example of a husband, treating his wife with respect. He remembers his father as someone who had a disability, but never, ever felt sorry for himself.

Archer firmly believes that growing up in Cassopolis, as small as it was and as poor as it was, was great for him. Between his parents and the people involved in his life, he was given the values upon which he bases his life today—values that he passed on to his sons and his grandsons. His father and mother taught him manners. They reminded him to say yes ma'am and no ma'am, yes sir and no sir before he walked out of the house. Some of the lessons seem simple, but they are arguably some of the most important lessons parents can teach their children. His father never saw him graduate from college or law school. He never saw Archer take on the responsibilities of being a husband and father. He didn't live to see his son become president of the American Bar Association or two-term Mayor of Detroit. Archer has a sense, however, that his father is with him, by his side, very much enjoying the life he has built from being a powerful political presence and change agent to his role as a husband and father. "Even though my dad did not have the financial wherewithal, he gave me the fundamentals that have allowed me to be who I am in terms of respecting people," says Dennis. "That in and of itself is the most important lesson he could have ever taught me."

Kim Harris Jones

Corporate Finance Executive

"I am certain who I am today is because of the lessons my father taught me and the love and support both my father and my mother provided every day."

Bloodlines and DNA do not always define fatherhood. It is sometimes so much more, especially when a loving, devoted father figure takes on responsibilities that some men would never dare. In times like these, a father's love—whether a stepfather, a grandfather, an uncle, or even a mentor—often transcends the classic definition of fatherhood. Corporate finance executive, Kim Harris Jones, finds herself in a unique position when discussing her relationship with her father. When she speaks of the man who loved, nurtured and guided her on a path toward greatness since the day she was born, she is referring to her legally adopted father, Fred "Chink" Harris.

Jones is the Chicago-based senior vice president, corporate controller of Mondelez International (formerly Kraft Foods) where she is responsible for all external financial reporting, and corporate planning and analysis. A finance and business expert with over twenty-five years of experience, Jones joined Kraft in June 2009 from Chrysler where she served as senior vice president, corporate controller, and auditor in a career that spanned seventeen years with the company. At Chrysler, Jones was the first African American female to be appointed vice president and also the first to serve as a corporate officer. Prior to Chrysler, Jones held a variety of finance leadership roles for General Motors, a company she went to work for upon graduating with an MBA from the University of Michigan's Stephen M. Ross School of Business. She began her career as senior auditor for Deloitte and Touche. Throughout her extraordinary career, Jones has served on several nonprofit boards and received numerous awards and honors including being named one of the 75 most powerful women in business by *Black Enterprise Magazine* and one of the 100 leading women by *Automotive News*. Jones is a certified public accountant, a lifetime member of the National Black MBA Association, and a member of the Executive Leadership Council. She attributes much of her success to the role her father played in her life.

Born February 14, 1960 in Detroit, Michigan, Jones didn't learn until she was a teenager that the dad she had loved dearly all her life was not her biological father. She and her older sisters and brother, who all grew up in the same house, share the same biological mother *and* father, but because she was the baby of the family and had been legally adopted by Fred at a very young age, many, including Kim, assumed Fred was her biological father. None of this mattered to Jones, however, because from the time she was born until the time of his death in 1987, Fred treated her as his very own and they shared an unbreakable father-daughter bond. She proudly refers to herself as "Daddy's Girl."

Fred Harris was born in 1919 in Mississippi and raised in Memphis, Tennessee, by his mother after his father died when he was just a young boy. Fred would share stories with Kim about his grandparents who were born into slavery. He also shared accounts of the poverty he endured and the racial discrimination he faced growing up in the Jim Crow South during the Great Depression. Fred was denied many opportunities and never viewed college as a viable option for a poor black kid from the south. He lost his thumb right after high school while working on a railroad. Because of his loss, he did not go to the military like many of his peers. Instead, armed with a high school diploma, Fred decided to leave Memphis for Detroit in the early 1950's after hearing of opportunities to work in the auto industry. He got a job on the General Motors assembly line—something he was extremely proud of. Some years later Fred met and married Velva Bass. Velva was divorced with four children, including her youngest child, Kim. Shortly after their marriage Fred legally adopted Kim.

Jones remembers her dad as a personable, kind man and recalls fondly how he helped her get through her very first day of kindergarten. Her father, who stood six feet three inches tall, was anxious about how his daughter would fare and decided to stay with her all day, sitting in one of the tiny chairs made especially for small children. Jones recalls being scared that first day of school and feeling so relieved and happy that her father didn't leave. Her friends who attended kindergarten with her still laugh at this heartwarming memory of her father's love.

From a very young age, Jones has been an early riser and a bona fide perfectionist, just like her father. On Saturday mornings, her parents would visit Detroit's famed Eastern Market, the largest historic commercial district in the U.S. where locally grown produce, flowers, meats, spices, and other goods are sold. Her father would leave the house early in the morning to head to Eastern Market, and if Jones wanted to join them she would have to get up before sunrise. On many weekends, her father would come into her bedroom at 7 o'clock in the morning and say, "Half the day is gone already!" Fred was a stickler for punctuality and attendance—he wasn't just on time, he was always really early for everything. Jones says she is exactly the same way about punctuality and to this day penalizes people on her staff by giving them extra assignments when they are late for her staff meetings. She hates being late and has to be pretty much incapacitated before she will miss a day of work. The one ironic thing about Fred's punctuality that Jones recalls is that her wedding got started about ten minutes late because they had to wait for her dad, overcome with emotion, to stop crying.

Most people who knew them both over the years have said, "Oh my god, you're just like your father." Her dad, one of the hardest working men Jones has ever known, was due to report to work each day at six o'clock in the morning, but he liked to get to work at 4:30. Jones recalls that her dad took a lot of pride in what he did and even received an award for never being absent in any of his more than thirty-year career with General Motors. His work ethic as a unionized assembly line worker was tremendous. His philosophy for his daughter was, "Always in whatever you do, I want you to do better, but whatever you do, you absolutely need to do your best." Hearing this as a child frustrated Jones, and she would get mad at her dad.

But in reality, she was the exact same way. In true perfectionist fashion, if Jones had a homework assignment and her paper somehow got wrinkled, her mother would iron the paper before she went to school. Jones could not stand to have anything out of place and her mother's goal each morning was to keep her calm and make sure she wasn't stressed before she went to school. If she didn't get an A in a class, she wouldn't be very happy and if she got a B she didn't want to show her father her report card at all. Jones recalls with laughter times when she brought her report card home with all A's. Her father would take his time reviewing the report card and, without acknowledging her stellar grades, would look at her attendance report and say, "Why were you absent a day?" or "Why were you late?" If she came home with anything less than all A's he would firmly remind her that she could do better and on those rare occasions that she came home with a B he'd say, "*You* know you can do better than this, and *I* know you can do better than this." This was his way of pushing Jones to work to the best of her abilities.

Jones admits that her father wasn't saying anything to her that she had not already said to herself because she was always pretty tough on herself. Nonetheless, her dad inspired her to work very hard. There were some classes, however, where she had to say to herself, "Hey, I did my best, and my best in this case didn't have to be an A." She realized and accepted the fact that she couldn't be perfect in everything, and from time to time she cut herself just a little bit of slack.

Whenever Jones was involved in an afterschool or evening activity, her father was right there with her greeting other parents with his usual outgoing and personable demeanor. The mothers of her fellow Girl Scouts knew Fred well. People would tell Jones, "You know, your father talks about you all the time." Her close relationship with her father and the many ways he showed how much he loved her has always stuck with her. Jones cherished her time with her father and knew that he adored her.

Fred taught his daughter lessons that have served her well over the years. He taught her that she must grow up to be an independent woman, fully capable of taking care of herself. Jones also saw a wonderful example of a very independent, self-assured woman in her mother, Velva. Seeing her mother work outside the home and raise four children served to reinforce her dad's lessons of independence. He taught her to do things for herself so that she would never need to depend on a man. This was one of his philosophies that influenced how Jones decided to live her life. She listened to his words, heeded his advice, and aspired to grow into a responsible, independent woman.

When it came to discipline in the Harris family, Velva was the parent who kept the kids in line, and despite the fact that Jones spent a lot of time with her father; she and her mom were still very close. Still, Velva raised her children with the "spare the rod spoil the child" approach. Jones can recall only one time in her life when her father motioned like he was going to spank her for fighting with her brother. "I looked at my father like he was crazy," Kim laughs. "I thought to myself, you've got to be kidding."

Because of his own upbringing with few financial resources and even fewer opportunities, Fred did everything within his power to make sure that his daughter understood the critical importance of education and saving for a solid financial future. He was adamant about Jones seizing every opportunity to get a world-class education and taught her to save money. Although he was initially skeptical of banks, he took Jones when she was just ten years old to open her first bank account at the National Bank of Detroit when a branch opened right near their home. Jones doesn't recall if her dad was the best saver, but he certainly tried to teach her the value of the almighty dollar.

Growing up, sometimes Jones suspected that the father she knew and loved might not be her biological father. When she learned that Fred was not her biological father, her response was, "Ok, I got it. I guess it's good to know." Admittedly, she was caught by surprise, but the news did not change her relationship with her dad in any way, nor did it change much about her relationship with her biological father. "Fred was the only father I had known and there was no reason to think he was *not* my father," Kim says. More than anything, it probably changed how she thought of her siblings. It made her think that perhaps if she had known, maybe she wouldn't have fought so much with her brother. Her brother was very close to their biological father who was pretty well to do. In retrospect, Jones feels that she used to get mad because her brother got all kinds of stuff from his dad, which made her somewhat jealous at times. Conversely, her older sisters and brother would get mad too because she was the baby of the family and Fred spoiled her rotten.

When it was time to make decisions about which college to attend, Jones decided early on that she was going to major in accounting and knew the University of Michigan had a great business school. She didn't want her academic pursuits to be too much of a financial strain on her family and felt that attending a highly ranked, in-state university would be a great fit for her. Both of her parents expressed concern about the scale of the university and whether or not she would be successful at a predominantly white institution. Jones assuaged their fears by doing well in school. As she matriculated, she received an esteemed award as a University of Michigan James B. Angell Scholar for consecutive semesters of all A's. Fred was incredibly proud of his daughter. In fact, every little thing she did made him proud. Any type of award she received, her dad would cheerfully display. He was so proud that he would talk with anyone who would listen about his daughter's many accomplishments. The attention embarrassed Jones at the time, but she knew unequivocally that it was all out of love. When she received recognition in college, it reaffirmed for her parents that she could thrive in this rigorous academic environment where few people looked like her.

Jones graduated from the University of Michigan in the spring of 1982 and went to work in public accounting for a company now known as Deloitte. While working at Deloitte, Kim became engaged to Jeffrey Jones. When Jones told her father she was getting married, he was afraid that she wouldn't pursue an advanced degree. Again, education was a non-negotiable for his daughter. She didn't disappoint her father and made good on an unspoken promise to continue her education. Kim married Jeffrey in 1984 and started the University of Michigan MBA program just a few months after the wedding. "Just because I got married didn't mean my education wasn't still a priority," Kim says.

Jones recalls two of the proudest moments in her father's life. One occurred when she graduated with her MBA from the University of Michigan and the second was when she took a job with General Motors. Coming out of the MBA program, Jones had several job offers. She told her father about an offer she received from General Motors and his immediate reaction was, "Why haven't you accepted it?"

Kim replied, "Well, you know I'm negotiating."

Her father said, "You better take that offer before they take it back."

When she finally accepted the position before she officially graduated from the Michigan MBA Program, her father had taken ill. Jones laughs to think that all of her father's friends told her they knew that she accepted the position at GM and what her salary would be. Her dear dad told his friends every detail about her brilliant achievements. She scolded her father: "Dad you can't tell all of my business."

Her father's reply: "Well, you shouldn't have told me."

Fred died of cancer the year after Kim began working for GM. Before he passed he expressed how immensely proud he was that she earned her MBA and was working for the company he devoted more than three decades of his life to.

When Jones first started with General Motors in 1986 she worked in a department where there were maybe one or two women, and none of the men in the department had wives that worked outside of the home. Some people in this predominantly white male-dominated environment had the perception that Jones has gotten the job because she was a woman or because she was African American. Her philosophy was and has always been: "Show them." She knew that she had reached a certain level of success because she was blessed, smart, determined and more than capable of doing the job. Her father would always say to her, "You have shown me that you can compete with the best, so don't let anybody think that you are a second-class citizen." When faced with stressful work situations, Jones pictures her father sitting in that tiny chair on her first day of kindergarten. This reminds her that although he isn't here physically, he is by her side making sure she's strong enough to withstand any challenges that come her way. She also vividly remembers that her family lived right in the area of the Detroit riots. She was seven years old when the riots broke out in 1967, and she recalls her father and uncle sitting on the front porch with shotguns protecting their house. She also remembers dealing with the death of her brother, who was murdered in a robbery attempt against him when she was twenty. In reflecting on the support from her father and some of the scary moments she has faced in life, she knows that if she can deal with these kinds of hardships, she can deal with anything.

Kim and Jeffrey, her husband of twenty-nine years, have two sons. She admits that her approach to parenting is different than that of her parents because she was raised in a stricter environment. Like her parents, they believe in stressing education and the importance of doing well. She loves that her father was a very integral part of her life when she was a girl, but even more important to her today is the fact that her husband is heavily involved in their boys' lives because boys need their fathers to teach them how to become responsible men. One of Jones's biggest regrets is that her sons never had a chance to meet their grandfather.

Through tears, Kim recalls a Luther Vandross song, "Dance with My Father," that touches her to her very core. When she hears the song, she remembers standing on her dad's feet, dancing around the room with him. Her dad never got the chance to witness many of

Jones's personal and professional accomplishments, but she believes there are milestones in her career where she can imagine her dad saying, "Job well done!" Jones did have a relationship with her biological father and learned that he had followed her successes and had also always been very proud of her, though from a distance. She feels very blessed to have had two fathers during her lifetime.

Jones talks to students about achieving professional success and remembers one speech she gave a few years ago to a consortium of graduate students. She shared with them her philosophy of what it takes to be successful and feels that all of the things she told them are consistent with life lessons from her father which include always giving your best, giving back, remaining humble and treating people the way you want to be treated.

Her father, Fred Harris, gave her the tools and the inspiration to excel at being the best person she could be. He paved the way for an extraordinary education and set the stage for Jones to have a better life than he had growing up. "Not that he thought he had a bad life," Kim explains. "He would say to me, 'I want you to absolutely do better than me,' and he and my mom provided me with the motivation, the inspiration and they were behind me every step of the way. That's what I think made a difference." Both her father and her mother encouraged her and were proud of everything she did. "Part of my success is driven by this: my God-given abilities coupled with having parents who encouraged me to be the best I can be," Kim explains. "I am certain who I am today is a result of the lessons my father taught me and the love and support both my father and my mother provided every day."

Stefan Holt

Television News Anchor

*"My dad taught me to work hard and laugh hard," Stefan says.
"You have to be able to laugh at yourself and others, and
sometimes at the absurdity of our world. That's going to get you
through the good times and the bad times."*

Stefan Holt is the witty, affable news anchor Chicagoans welcome into their homes as they sip their morning cup of coffee. There's something remarkably familiar about his comfortable style and his measured cadence as he delivers the first news of the day in the nation's third largest media market. His eyes have the faint resemblance of eyes we've trusted for years. And that smile. Yes, we've definitely seen that smile before. Holt is the son of veteran broadcast journalist, Lester Holt, co-host of the weekend editions of NBC's *The Today Show* and *Nightly News*. The elder Holt also serves as host of the NBC's venerable newsmagazine program *Dateline*.

Like his father, twenty-five-year-old Holt found his passion in news. He graduated cum laude from Pepperdine University with a Bachelor's degree in broadcast telecommunications and political science. While studying on the west coast, Holt anchored and reported for Malibu's only local news station, NewsWaves 26. He also produced and anchored the news for 101.5 KWVS, the Pepperdine University radio station. Holt worked as a correspondent for the college network, Palestra.net, where he was on the front line during the 2007 Southern California wildfires when smoke and flames came onto the Pepperdine campus. Holt's reports covering the school's evacuation were seen on FOX News Channel and MSNBC. After college, he got his official start in news on WPBF in West Palm Beach, Florida, where he covered everything from tropical storms to gas station robberies, even demonstrating some impressive dance moves on the heels of a report that claimed men who can dance are more attractive to women. Not for his dance moves but for his extraordinary journalism skills, Holt got the attention of the Chicago NBC affiliate and landed a job with WMAQ reporting from the field and manning the weekend anchor desk. In February 2012, Holt was promoted to the high-profile weekday morning anchor desk making his dad mighty proud.

Holt's dad, Lester Don Holt Jr., is the youngest of four children. He was born on an Air Force base in 1959 and grew up in northern California and Alaska. Holt reflects on tales of his dad having a really rich childhood that contributed to his love for journalism. As a young kid, his father wanted to be a Top 40 DJ. Lester would also play news reporter and pretend to be pioneer broadcast journalist, Walter Cronkite. When he was ten years old, he sat in front of the television watching in amazement as Neil Armstrong, the commander of the

Apollo 11 spacecraft, took the first step on the moon, thereby transforming human exploration. Lester was perplexed, however, that there weren't any African American anchors on television to report arguably the most monumental moment in the history of mankind.

Lester graduated from Cordova High School in Ranchero Cordova, California in 1977 and studied government at California State University in Sacramento. While in college he landed a job as a country and western disc jockey at a local radio station. Station management eventually moved Lester from the late night country and western show to reporting news around Sacramento. He fell in love with news and even bought a police radio scanner to find out what was happening around the city. Later he moved to San Francisco where he got a job at KCBS Radio. There, Lester met the lovely Carol Hagen from Seattle. They married in 1981 and moved to New York where he was hired as a reporter for WCBS-TV. In 1982, he became a reporter and weekend anchor on KNXT in Los Angeles, and the next year he returned to WCBS-TV as a reporter and weekend anchor. In 1986, Lester and Carol moved to Chicago where he anchored the evening news for WBBM-TV. Their sons, Stefan and Cameron were both born in Chicago.

Holt has always admired his father's ability to strike a healthy work-life balance and spend quality time with his family. Whenever he or his brother had activities before school, his father would get up with them. He cooked breakfast, walked the boys to school, and even took the time to coach their flag football or baseball teams. "I remember having family dinners as a kid which was difficult because my dad worked in the evenings," Stefan says. "He had a break between the six o'clock news and the ten o'clock news. He would come home, spend some time with us and then jump back in the car to go back to work."

Now that he's older, Holt realizes the sacrifices his father made. He also respects that his dad has never been afraid to show affection especially because hugs seemed prohibited among some of his friends and their dads. He remembers a time when his father returned home from a business trip and picked him up from school. Elated to have his dad home, Holt gave him the biggest hug he could muster right in front of all of his friends, symbolic of how much love they have always shared. Holt's friends gave him a hard time: "You hug your dad like that in front of everybody?" Holt told his friends to back off and remembers thinking how cool it was that he and his dad weren't afraid to show the world that they have a really good relationship. His dad thought it was cool too.

Over the years father and son have spent a good amount of time talking news, politics, sports and debating about what's going on in the world. Holt reveals that his dad has always had a wicked sense of humor and is a naturally funny guy. He appreciates that his dad is a big practical joker. April Fool's Day one year was particularly brutal in the Holt household. He and his brother were just waking up to get ready for school when their dad walked in Holt's room holding the telephone. Pretending to have a conversation with someone he said, "What? The whole school is closed due to a water main break?" The boys high fived each other and with smiles on their faces, went to their rooms and pulled the covers over their heads preparing to fall back into a deep, satisfying slumber. Lester had them going for a long time that morning, finally yelling "April Fools!" They jumped up with scowls on their faces and rushed to get dressed and head to school. Holt had to admit to his dad that he got them. "Good one, Dad" Stefan yelled to his father as he hurried into the school building.

Family time has always been important to the Holt family. Mendocino, a quaint little town in northern California that Lester and Carol discovered many years ago, became one of their favorite places to visit. In Mendocino, they were able to enjoy breathtaking views of the Pacific Ocean. The family would go on hikes together and explore the great outdoors. They spent time reading plenty of books, playing board games, and completely unplugging from the rest of the world. Today, it's more difficult for the family to travel together due to hectic work and travel schedules, but the time they do spend together is cherished. Holt, his dad and his brother, Cameron, are all die-hard Ping-Pong players and perhaps competitive to a fault. Holt admits that Cameron and his father are better at the game and sometimes he gets knocked out of the competition. For bragging rights, his dad and brother will duke it out, pounding that little white Ping-Pong ball for hours.

Holt has always seen his father as a role model and has never wanted to disappoint him. His dad taught him to own up to his mistakes and not be afraid to apologize. Both of his parents had high expectations that their sons would do well in school. As Holt looks back on his childhood, he remembers writing papers that his dad would help him with and critique. "Where does your argument stand?" his dad would ask. Always a skillful writer and an exceptional wordsmith, Lester would challenge his son to be a strong writer. In addition to writing, Holt was always taught to be clear and concise when communicating and to always speak up. From these valuable lessons, he learned to think critically and write effectively—lessons that undoubtedly serve him well in his profession.

In 2000, Lester accepted the position at NBC and the family moved from Chicago to New York. For thirteen-year-old Holt, the move from Chicago, the city he knew and loved, to New York was tough. He was born in Chicago, went to school in Chicago, and had always been a huge Chicago Bears fan. Holt was not the kind of kid to complain and he thought back on his dad's life and all of the moving he did as the child of a sergeant in the U.S. Air Force. Because his father had once walked in his shoes, he confirmed for Stefan that everything would work out just fine. Holt tried in earnest to figure out New York City, which, for him, had a totally different vibe than Chicago. Chicago had more of a laidback feel to young Holt, who enjoyed playing football in Chicago's Lincoln Park or bike riding with friends along Lake Michigan's famed bike path that stretches for miles along the city skyline. In New York, everything felt larger than life and the city moved at a frenzied pace. He had to learn to adjust and quicken his own pace for everything from walking through the streets of Manhattan to figuring out which kids in his new class he could befriend.

Eventually he settled in to his new city, and the move turned out to be really good for the family.

His dad's elation over his new job was palpable, and Holt was just as excited for the elder Holt. He remembers going to the *Today Show* studios with his dad to soak it all in and hang out in the television news environment that would one day become "home" for him too. Sitting at the anchor desk just minutes before the show went live was a surreal feeling for Stefan. He would walk the halls of NBC and chat with Bryant Gumbel and Katie Couric, two of the biggest names in television news. The producers would throw young Holt a headset and let him cue the opening of the show. He would conduct mock interviews with his brother in his father's office. These experiences helped him realize how fascinating news was to him. Holt believed his father had the best of both worlds. "A little bit of fun and a little bit of seriousness. I know he loved it and still does," Stefan says. "My dad works long hours, and it's a big chunk of his weekend, but he's living a broadcaster's dream. He's doing the job he always wanted to do." His father's tireless dedication and incredible work ethic have set a strong example for both Holt boys—a work ethic Holt has tried to emulate with his own style and flavor, of course. "Despite my dad's work schedule, we truly valued those family times, and we still do," Stefan says. "We were still able to have a relationship, and I am remarkably close to my dad and even closer now that we are in the same business."

In addition to news, Holt and his dad share a love for aviation and all things involving flight. He holds fond memories of spending time with his dad at the Chicago Air and Water Show and building model airplanes side by side. Father and son would spend hours talking about airplanes. They would also watch planes land at O'Hare International Airport where they would pick up Holt's mom, who worked as a flight attendant. "What kind of airplane is that, a "747 or 757?" his father would ask. They could even tell the difference by the sound of the airplane. "It's funny, but even today my dad will send me an email now that says, 'Hey, did you see this picture of the new Boeing 787?'" Holt shares.

Holt's grandfather, Lester Sr., learned to fly as a kid, and became a private pilot after serving in the Air Force. His paternal uncle is an airline pilot who also served in the Air Force. Holt remembers going up for a demonstration flight just after high school. He fell head over heels in love with flying, and he knew right then that he wanted to fly. The summer between his freshmen and sophomore year in college, Holt worked as a busboy making close to minimum wage plus tips to pay for expensive flight lessons. He worked from four o'clock in the afternoon to midnight, and then he would wake up early the next morning at five a.m. to fly all day long and go right back to work. His parents were very supportive, and his dad knew it was something he was working hard to accomplish on his own. He earned his pilot's license in 2006 just after his freshmen year in college.

During his very first flight as a private pilot, he flew his parents around Manhattan, down the Hudson River and past the

Statue of Liberty. Being at the controls and flying his parents around Manhattan was a proud moment for Holt. After he got them back on the ground safely, he remembers his father telling people, "My son just flew me around. That's pretty cool!"

When Holt first broke into news, he and his dad were competitors. Holt was on the ABC *Weekend Morning Show* in West Palm Beach, Florida. Lester was on the NBC *Morning Show*. "It was funny because if you had two TV's next to one another, I'd be on one and my dad would be on the other," Stefan says. Today, father and son both work for NBC but even when they worked for competing networks, his father was, and continues to be, Holt's most important mentor. Holt respects everything his dad does, not only as a father, but also as one of the best broadcasters in the business. Being fortunate enough to grow up under his dad's tutelage has meant more to Holt than his dad will ever fully realize. He feels that he has had an incredible education in broadcasting and journalism and his dad has always been there for him. "I value his opinion and his critique of my work, not only as someone with thirty years of experience in the business but also as a father looking out for his son." Stefan says.

As a young broadcast journalist who's been on the news desk for just a few years, Holt is still soaking everything in and working hard to hit his stride. His father has been brutally honest with Holt about the industry and all of the changes—both good and bad—he has seen in the last three decades. The elder Holt offered that if he works hard, enjoys what he does, and strives to be the best, he will have a very rewarding and fulfilling career. For Holt, now almost four years in, it has been exactly as his father described.

Returning to Chicago in 2011 to work for the local NBC affiliate has been a welcome homecoming for Holt. Just thinking about his return to his hometown reminds him of the day his family left Chicago to move to New York. He remembers sitting in the backseat with the whole family piled in the car, dogs and all. As his dad drove out of Chicago heading south on the Dan Ryan Expressway, he watched the city skyline slip off in the distance. Holt remembers it being a sad but adventurous time as they drove the more than 700 miles to the Big Apple to settle into their new lifestyle on the East Coast.

Fast-forward twelve years. Stefan and Morgan, his girlfriend at the time, were driving from Florida to Chicago. They entered the Dan Ryan Expressway, that familiar expressway that brings you into the heart of the city. He remembers seeing the city's skyline ushering him back to all that he knew and loved. He never dreamed that he would return to Chicago to work and much to his delight, he received a warm reception from old friends and viewers who watch him every morning. "Chicagoans are great because they admire and respect people who are from the streets they are from," Stefan says. "It's great to be back." He admits that being a morning anchor is tough, particularly adjusting to the hours. His alarm clock goes off at one thirty or two o'clock in the morning and though rising that early is still a struggle, he finds something incredibly rewarding about having the opportunity to look up in the camera and tell Chicagoans what's going on in the city and the world. And he is comforted knowing that his father is in New York feeling the same way about his work.

Despite his father's travel and long work hours, his mom, whom he considers pretty savvy, does incredibly well and has been incredibly supportive. Holt recounts a recent time when he sent his mom a text to check on her when his father was away on assignment. Understandably, Carol worries about her husband as he covers devastating storms like super storm Sandy in the fall of 2012. "She gets nervous because that is her sweetheart being blown around in the rain and wind. At least she can check on him. She turns on NBC and there he is," Stefan says. His father was in Afghanistan during a recent Thanksgiving. As a family, they all knew he had a job to do and they watched him on the air telling the story of American soldiers in Afghanistan who couldn't be home for Thanksgiving. In a sense, Holt, his mother and brother found some comfort knowing that Lester was able to provide a voice for those overseas. In those moments, of which there have been many, Holt gives thanks that his father's career as a journalist allows him to impact so many lives.

Holt describes the relationship between his father and mother as very affectionate. Holt remembers his parents having date nights every now and then. After he and his brother moved out of the nest, Lester and Carol even started taking Italian classes together. "They are cute together," Stefan laughs. "They complement each other nicely." To Holt, his parents have represented an extraordinary model for what a loving relationship should be. He feels they are great parents and even better spouses.

In July 2012 Holt married his longtime love, Morgan, whom he met while they were both undergraduate students at Pepperdine. His dad had to be in London to cover the Summer Olympics but moved heaven and earth to organize his schedule so that he could be in Malibu, California for his son's wedding. While in Malibu, father and son had the chance to hang out and spend some very meaningful time together, even sharing a room for part of the week. In their quiet moments, Holt and his dad did a lot of talking and laughing. They talked mostly about marriage and life in general, but managed to sneak in a bit of shoptalk too.

Holt has learned a myriad of lessons from his father through the years. "My dad taught me to work hard and laugh hard, and these are two things I hope to pass on to my kids," Stefan says. "You have to be able to laugh at yourself and others, and sometimes at the absurdity of our world. That's going to get you through the good times and the bad times."

Holt also relishes the spiritual values he has learned from his dad. Lester is a very spiritual, very religious man, and Holt, too, adopted many of his father's spiritual beliefs growing up watching how his father approached spirituality. Now that they are in the same business, he realizes how important the spiritual aspect of their lives is. "My dad and I have to cover and report on a lot of devastation and sadness but having a firm spiritual foundation carries you through at the end of the day." His father taught him the importance of trusting in the Lord and understanding that it's not always up to you—a lesson he also plans to pass onto his kids.

Thanks to his dad, and the upstanding ways he has molded and shaped the values of both of his sons, Holt looks forward to being a father some day and he is not ashamed to say that he wants to be the same kind of father to his kids that his dad has been. Until then, Holt gets a kick out of being "in the business" and occasionally tossing to the elder Holt as he's doing a live report on *The Today Show*. "I'm kind of goofy about it, and I find it surreal working for the same company as my dad and handing off a story to him. I call him dad on the air too which catches a lot of people off guard," Stefan says, laughing.

Yvette D. Clarke

United States Congresswoman

"It's a delightful feeling to know that my father, who invested a lot of time in my brother and me, gets to see the dividends of his tireless work as a father. And we get to experience it together."

Never has there been a more determined, focused, and spirited public servant than Yvette Diane Clarke. Congresswoman Clarke has answered to several titles including activist, community organizer, and now legislator in the Brooklyn community where she has lived and worked most of her life. But to the man who has nurtured her fervent spirit, she simply answers to daughter. Clarke is known for her boldness, compassion and love for humanity, all of which have contributed to her becoming an effective leader and an outspoken advocate on numerous issues of great importance to her constituents—especially her father who is perhaps her staunchest critic and her biggest ally.

In 2006, she became the youngest African American woman to serve in the United States Congress, taking the seat first occupied by the late Honorable Shirley Chisholm, the first African American woman elected to Congress more than forty years ago.

Clarke serves New York's 11th Congressional District with an extraordinary sense of pride and loyalty. When she is on the Floor of the U.S. House of Representatives working through a piece of legislation, Clarke doesn't have to try very hard to conjure up her father's sage advice. "My father calls me," she laughs. Her phone will ring and immediately she'll recognize her father's voice. "Yvette, please tell President Obama…"

She'll stop him and jokingly say, "Hold on Dad, I'm going to put the president on three-way right now." She loves that her father cares about her work as a politician and is grateful that they share such a close relationship.

Clarke, born November 21, 1964, is proud to be a Brooklyn native with roots firmly planted in her Jamaican heritage. Her father, Leslie Lloyd Clarke, Sr., was born and raised in Kingston. Her mother, Una Sylvia Tomlinson Clarke, was born in St. Elizabeth. The young couple, ambitious, eager to further their education, and filled with hope for the future, came to the United States as foreign students during a time of tremendous political and social change. Una entered the United States in 1958 and, after their wedding in Jamaica, Leslie arrived in 1959. Together, they stood for social justice from the moment they called Brooklyn home.

When Clarke was a young girl, her family was an integral part of the Brooklyn community fighting for social justice. She recalls when her father, who worked as a civil engineer, would put his construction hat on her small head and lift her high in the air. Perched on her father's strong shoulders, she had a bird's eye view during rallies and protests, and she felt safe. She recalls periods of time when police brutality created a crisis in their community. In 1976, a ninth-grader, Randolph Evans, was shot and killed at the Cypress Hills Housing Project by an NYPD officer. Clarke remembers the whole community coming out to protest his untimely death in front of the 75th Precinct. The shooting officer was eventually arrested and indicted. Coming out to raise their collective voices was the type of civic responsibility and social justice that Clarke learned from her father and mother at a very young age. It became a blueprint for her life as a community activist and later as a legislator. Her dad, without fail, provided wisdom, guidance, and direction, and encouraged meaningful participation in such community protests and events. As the protector of the family, he was instrumental in shaping the family's values and instilling in Clarke, the belief that she was put on this earth to help change the world in a positive way. These values have stayed with her and she feels fortunate to have grown up in an active household where community organizing and activism were alive and well.

The idea of public service was a feeling that was always present in their lives. Her parents, because they were immigrants, tried to find ways to first understand, then to navigate the American system by learning as much about it as they could. So much so that when Clarke and her brother were young, both parents became heavily involved in the local Parent-Teacher Association. They quickly became adept at all issues regarding public education and made their children's education a main focus. Clarke recalls that her mother, a proud pioneer and long-time advocate for child welfare, education, health and mental health and economic development, delved into politics as a natural progression of her concern for the community and her spirit of activism. Una preceded her daughter on the New York City Council, making the Clarke women the first mother-daughter succession in the history of the council.

Her father taught his children that being well educated in the United States was the pathway to success. Leslie earned a Bachelor's degree from Brooklyn's Pratt Institute and completed additional postgraduate work. For over forty years, Leslie worked for the Port Authority of New York and New Jersey, first as a civil engineer, and later as an architect. Her father held other jobs while earning his undergraduate degree, including working as a disc jockey on the night shift at a local radio station when Clarke was very young. Even with going to school and working long hours, Leslie remained vigilant about his children's education and going over homework with Clarke was most important to him. Leslie loved teaching his children about current events. Clarke recalls being glued to the television screen for an entire week in 1977 watching and discussing with her dad, mom and brother, Alex Haley's *Roots*, the historic mini series depicting several generations in the lives of a slave family. She also remembers sitting at the kitchen table with her father discussing politics.

Inasmuch as he loved engaging his children in discussions about hot button issues, Leslie also spent time joking and laughing with them, and treating his little girl like a princess. On hot summer days when the ice cream truck came rolling down their tree-lined Brooklyn street, her dad was the person she would go to for money to buy ice cream. And if the ice cream truck went by before she could make her plea, she would surreptitiously figure out a way to get him to take her to her favorite ice cream shop, Carvel. Clarke has always had a special touch with her dad that she coyly refers to as "having him wrapped around my finger."

She describes her father as a disciplinarian, acknowledging that discipline was important in their family. She recalls receiving spankings from her parents, but their disappointment is what upset her the most. Clarke was always strong-willed and eager to push the envelope. Her father had a "three strikes and you're out" rule, but Clarke constantly tested the boundaries and inevitably got to three and a half strikes. Her mother was just as much of a disciplinarian as her dad, but she didn't want to be seen that way. Clarke recalls an animated television program where the mother would yell: "Wait until your father gets home!" something her own mother would say regularly. On these occasions, she would finish the dishes and go to bed before dark just to mute her father's level of disappointment. Her parents were very much into shaping respectful children and would discipline their children physically if they were potentially putting themselves in harm's way or if they did not follow the rules.

The Clarkes were a working-class family, yet Yvette never once felt financial pressures because her dad and mom created a space for their children filled with love and deep concern for their well being. She didn't pick up on the fact that her parents had to make very careful financial choices until she was much older. When, trying to fit in with her peers, Clarke would ask her parents for a new pair of Jordache jeans or Adidas sneakers, and they would buy the generic brand. Whatever her parents bought, no matter the cost, was presented to her with love.

Although her parents have lived in the United States longer than they lived in Jamaica, they still have Jamaican accents. Her father, however, insisted that Clarke and her brother speak proper English. While she taught her father street slang and what was going on in the neighborhood, she also feels that she taught him patience and not to be so judgmental. Her parents grew up in Jamaica under British rule in a society that, according to Yvette, based judgments on an individual's status as an indicator of where he or she will end up in life. "They would make the distinction of who they would associate with based on the person's socioeconomic status; whereas, when you attend public schools in the United States, particularly in the community where I grew up, which was working class, you can't necessarily look at people's station in life," Yvette shares. She taught her father to be more open to the fact you will meet and make friends from all walks of life because their status doesn't diminish the type of relationship you can have with them. Over time she has seen her dad evolve to embrace those values.

Clarke attended Edward R. Murrow High School in the Midwood section of Brooklyn. She had to take a subway to get to school, and there was an overlapping period where her brother, Leslie, Jr., was responsible for her until he went off to Temple University. "To this day he thinks he is still responsible for me," Yvette says, laughing. She felt that her parents were overly protective but in retrospect, she understands why. At the time, however, it was clear to her that her peers were given a lot more latitude than she. Clarke remembers having to arrange outings with her brother including school dances. She even went to the high school prom with her brother's best friend.

In 1982, after graduating from high school, Clarke earned a scholarship to Oberlin College in Ohio and was a recipient of the prestigious APPAM/Sloan Fellowship in Public Policy and Policy Analysis. Leslie and Una agreed to send her away to college in Ohio, although it took some coaxing. She completed most of her education at Oberlin before returning to New York and subsequently earning a Bachelor's degree from Medgar Evers College.

When she returned from Ohio, she moved back home briefly but at that stage she relished her freedom. She eventually moved back to Flatbush, not to her parent's home but to a second home they owned on the same block, becoming their tenant for all intents and purposes. Clarke still lives in the quaint Flatbush home on Midwood Street today. "Dad is the main guy with house-related matters. I get to wrap him around my finger there too," she admits with a smile.

Being extremely meticulous and analytical are two of her dad's qualities that Clarke inherited—qualities that serve her well in her political career. "I analyze things to a pinhead, and I got that from my dad," Yvette says. "Having his drafting boards in the house and watching him work late into the night on schematics rubbed off on me. I am by no means the type of architect he is, but I build a certain type of architecture in my thinking to develop policies on behalf of the people I represent to move the agenda forward."

Always dad first, Leslie remains engaged in politics and concerned about what's going on in his daughter's congressional office. He even calls to make suggestions about how her press office should respond to newspaper articles she is mentioned in. She loves that her father is engaged and keeps in mind that his perspective is also as a member of the voting public. After all, her father and mother live in her constituency. They are voters who get information from different places in their Brooklyn community and share it with her. Most times her father's feedback is welcome. Clarke takes the not-so-welcome feedback in stride because she respects her father and appreciates the closeness they share. She tries to involve her parents in a lot of things because she cherishes these precious years, as her parents are getting older.

The times when her father has escorted her to a holiday party at the White House or a high profile political function in New York, Clarke notes that, dressed in his finest suit, her dad walks with his shoulders squared and a little extra pep in his step. She and her father still dance together a lot at events. And when he is in the audience during one of her public speeches that prompts a standing ovation, she sees her father standing in the front row with his chest rising to his chin. "Other people may not interact with their fathers as much as I do. Some folks are estranged from their fathers, but this is the way I was raised. I haven't departed from it."

Her father's extraordinary focus on education, and the love and wisdom he shares has challenged Clarke to become the person she is today. The life lessons he taught her have given her courage to face obstacles as the youngest African American woman to hold a position in Congress. She sees her father as a courageous man—a man of honor, dignity and integrity and he often tells her just how proud she has made him. "I think he feels that all of the work he put in helping to raise me has paid off," she says. "It's a delightful feeling to be around my parents and to know that my father, who invested a lot of time in my brother and me, gets to see the dividends of that. And we get to experience it together." Yvette says. "That is a great feeling."

Allan Houston

Philanthropist and NBA Star

"When I played in the NBA, people in the professional ranks of basketball—from referees and coaches, from managers to players—would say that my dad is one of the classiest men they've ever met. For me, this is just very consistent with the example he set and what I saw growing up."

When true basketball enthusiasts speak of Allan Houston, the label pure shooter typically spills from their lips as they pay homage to the two-time NBA All-Star's phenomenal shooting game. Some of today's NBA greats might argue that their baseline turnaround jumper is better than Houston's, but very few can prove it. With unrivaled focus and dedication, he brought an extraordinary work ethic to his venerable twelve-year NBA career, finishing as one of the league's all-time greatest long-range shooters and one of the all-time leading scorers in Knicks history. As a preeminent figure in basketball, he demonstrated a sense of maturity and selflessness that eludes many players. He was recognized for four straight years as one of *The Sporting News'* "Good Guys in Sports" and helped Team USA bring home the gold medal in the 2000 Summer

Olympic games in Sydney, Australia. But for all of his on the court success, Houston's extraordinary work off the court makes him a distinguished figure in the civic and philanthropic communities.

Houston, now forty-two, is in the second phase of his basketball career as the New York Knicks' assistant general manager. He is also principal and co-founder of the Allan Houston Legacy Foundation, a non-profit entity with year-round programming that focuses on family, mentoring, and relationship building between fathers and their children. Houston was named father of the year by the National Fatherhood Initiative in 2007. In 2011 he received the President's Council on Service and Civic Engagement Award from President Barack Obama's administration.

Houston is especially proud to have his father and mentor, Allan Wade Houston, Sr., by his side as a member of the Allan Houston Legacy Foundation management team and his de facto wingman. Houston's father has fueled his love for basketball and his desire to succeed since he first picked up a basketball at age six. He draws from the life lessons his father taught him and looks to his father for advice on how to make the greatest impact in the lives of countless families. To understand where Houston's extraordinary sense of integrity, exemplary values and overall greatness comes from, one only needs to peer into the window of his father's life to witness an undeniable legacy of leadership.

Wade Houston was born in 1944 and grew up in a close-knit, working-class family in Alcoa, Tennessee. Wade's father, Charlie Wade Houston, worked in the local aluminum plant until an illness forced his retirement in 1983 after over forty years of loyal service. During his years at the plant, Charlie experienced layoffs and work stoppages. To fill the financial gaps, he did janitorial work and held odd jobs to provide for his family. Witnessing his father's difficult times, Wade decided at a very early age that he would do whatever it took to control his financial future. He wanted to ensure his children would never have to see him struggle the way his father sometimes did.

Wade loved sports from the time he was a young boy. He played little league baseball, and his dad was also a big baseball fan. Wise beyond his years, he knew at an early age that his future success depended on studying and understanding more than just the fundamentals of basketball or baseball. He needed to learn the business of sports and he set out to do just that in addition to becoming a force to be reckoned with on the basketball court. Wade graduated from Charles M. Hall High School in 1962 and became the first African American basketball player to earn a scholarship to the University of Louisville. He graduated in 1966 and in 1970, traveled overseas to Strasbourg, France to play professional basketball. His wife, Alice Carolyn Kean Houston, became pregnant with Allan, their first child, while the young couple lived in France. Alice wanted to return to the United States to have the baby with her family close by. Wade and Alice later had two more children, daughters Lynn and Natalie.

After playing in Europe, Wade decided to pursue a Master's degree in educational psychology from the University of Louisville with his sights set on becoming a basketball coach. After graduate school, he began what would become a celebrated coaching career. Wade guided the Male High School basketball team to two state tournaments and won the 1974-1975 Kentucky state basketball championship. In 1975, when Houston was just four years old, his dad began a thirteen-year affiliation with the University of Louisville as an assistant coach under head coach, Danny Crum. During Wade's tenure, the University of Louisville's basketball teams appeared in four Final Four competitions, winning the national championship in both 1980 and 1986.

In the midst of building a tremendous legacy as a college coach, Wade never lost sight of his most important job—being a husband and father. To this day, Houston cherishes the times with his dad growing up. He recalls sitting on the couch when he was a young kid watching boxing while his dad cut his hair. He also remembers that his father wasn't afraid to give him a hug, show affection, and tell him, "I love you." These experiences with his father fueled Houston's confidence and taught him that he had to look no further than his own family to feel loved and supported. "He's very humble man who doesn't have to say a lot, but whatever he said, it's like gold because he backs it up with his actions," Allan says.

As a standout high school player, Houston had his sights set on playing college basketball for his father. During his senior year, Houston signed a commitment letter to the University of Louisville where his dad was assistant coach. He was thrilled to have a chance to fulfill his dream of playing college ball for his father, but in a twist of fate, months later Coach Houston was named head coach of the University of Tennessee's basketball program, making him the first black head coach in the Southeastern Conference (SEC).

Houston will never forget the moment his mother shared the good news with the family about his dad's new coaching job. He was happy for his dad and also felt a bit of panic because he had committed to Louisville. Wade later explained to his son that he wanted him to stay in Louisville if the NCAA planned to penalize him by making him sit out for a year. The family put it in God's hands. They prayed literally all summer for a favorable NCAA decision that would allow Houston to play four years of college basketball at Tennessee without losing a year of eligibility. This was important to Wade because he wanted his son to graduate and get his degree. The NCAA granted Houston four years of eligibility with no penalty for deciding to play for his dad at Tennessee without having to lose a year. The Houston family knew long before this time of adversity that God was on their side, but this unexpected blessing certainly reaffirmed it.

When Coach Houston arrived in Knoxville, Tennessee to begin his head coaching job, he was immediately reminded that being the SEC's first black head basketball coach would not erase decades of bigotry and racism. Houston will never forget his father's disappointment when a Knoxville country club that customarily grants memberships to the University of Tennessee's football and basketball coaches, made a public statement that they were not going to give the new head basketball coach a membership. This experience set the tone for what his father was stepping into and what he, as a player, would have to endure. Wade had to deal with the incredible pressure of being a head coach from dealing with praise and criticism from the media and the fans to navigating the complex dynamics of the athletic department. Houston was able to see from the inside just how the pressure affected his father.

To see Wade face blatant discrimination when hostile crowds yelled racial slurs was a difficult lesson for Houston, but it taught him a great deal about his father's character. Going to small southern towns where bigotry loomed large and playing in front of racist fans was difficult for him not only as a player but also as the son of the head coach. "Just going to Starkville, Mississippi and sensing the tension and hearing stuff about my dad was tough, but it fueled me a lot too," Allan says. "I combated this negativity by turning my level up a little bit because I wanted him to succeed." Houston admits, however, that he wasn't mature enough spiritually or emotionally to forgive and get past it. He held on to a lot of anger during his time as a University of Tennessee Volunteer, but he knew he had to put his anger aside and get the job done on the court.

During Houston's sophomore year in 1991, the Volunteers played extremely well in the SEC tournament and made it to the championship game. At the end of one of those memorable games, Houston went up and hugged his dad. This moment stands out for him because it summarized everything they had gone through that season—all of the hardships as well as the sanguine moments. "I just remember that embrace being real cool because we won the game and games in the tournament when we weren't expected to," Allan reflects. "I never felt closer to my father."

As a coach, Houston's father was never a yeller or a screamer, but he would always motivate the team, Houston especially, by challenging them mentally. The elder Houston cared about all of the young men on his team, from their growth and performance on the court, to the decisions they made off the court. Naturally, pleasing his father was important to Houston, and he wanted to make sure he represented his family in the right way. He didn't want to be the guy slouching in practice or getting caught doing something he wasn't supposed to do. "This was a challenge because I was a nineteen-year-old young man trying to explore manhood and my dad was the coach," Allan admits. "There were lots of times when I didn't want to let him down, but I still wanted to be a young man." On the court, Houston felt his father's presence both as a coach and as a father. It lifted and empowered him, and he felt his father's greatness every day. Houston also knew without question that his father would get on him in practice when he wasn't at the top of his game.

There was a time when Houston didn't do well in a class and his father made him sit out and miss the beginning of practice for weeks. While this may have embarrassed him, it sent Houston a powerful message that he was not bigger than the game, nor was he bigger than his education. "It wasn't that I didn't try to do well in this class," Allan explains. "But my dad told me, 'Look, it doesn't matter what the reason is, you've got to get it right,'" The experience, albeit a painful one, taught him that his father set a very high standard and would take drastic measures to make sure he excelled on the court and in the classroom. It taught him that he could waste time and energy making excuses about a tough class or an unrelenting professor, but in his father's eyes excuses were unacceptable. His father taught him to be prepared and accountable. Houston knew what he had to do because other than his spiritual growth, this was the most important lesson he would learn at this time in his young life.

In February 2011, when Houston's University of Tennessee jersey was retired, it was very emotional for father and son. It was the first time they were back on the University of Tennessee's basketball court together. As the 21,678 fans in attendance stood to salute Houston as one of the all-time greatest Volunteers, it was apropos that his entire family stood beside him: his father, mother, sisters, wife, Tamara, and children. During this time, he reflected on how his father handled his players and mostly, how he handled him. He felt his father's love during his years at Tennessee, just as he does now. Houston reflects that those four years were extremely critical and to a great degree, helped him develop into the man he has become.

Looking back on his dad's coaching career, Houston describes him as magnetic. "People were naturally drawn to him," Allan says. "My father studies people when he first meets them, but he is always easygoing and a good conversationalist—a skill he developed when he was a top basketball recruiter. Those who get to know him understand that he has a good sense of humor and likes to play practical jokes." In the four years that Houston played for his dad, he watched his father closely. He got to see his father's true character. Throughout Houston's career in the NBA, people in the professional ranks of basketball—from referees to coaches, from managers to players—never ceased to ask how his dad was doing, offering that he was one of the classiest men they ever met. For Houston, these kind words about his father rang true. He was blessed to watch and learn from his father how to live a life of integrity, no matter the circumstance. In 2003, Houston established the Wade Houston Scholarship at the University of Tennessee in honor of his father. The scholarships are awarded to deserving undergraduate African American students.

When Houston was drafted by the Detroit Pistons in the first round of the 1993 NBA draft, he went right into the league with the mentality of serving others, a lesson he learned from his father. Wade had always been very active in mentoring throughout Houston's life. "When he's not even trying to mentor actively, he is still mentoring," explains Allan. The NBA rookie already knew that "To whom much is given, much is required." This was something his father and mother exemplified and taught each of the three Houston children. "My parents made a big difference with the principles they taught us and the faith they instilled in us. They are true warriors of the work ethic." Fast forward to 2001 when tragedy struck on September 11. It occurred to Houston that a lot of kids were going to wake up without fathers. He knew that he could not be a silent observer or simply pray this tragedy away. It was time to ask God to use him so that he could begin serving others in a much more substantial way. Houston and his wife, Tamara, immediately started a fund to help some of the families who lost loved ones that day. The more they opened their hearts and lived the creed his father had instilled in him, the more they began to get pulled in different directions by different organizations. In lieu of writing checks to disparate non-profits, they decided to step back to talk about their goals and map out a philanthropic strategy that would have the greatest impact.

Houston, along with his dream team of advisors—his wife and parents—knew he wanted to equip young minds from an educational perspective and support and uplift fathers. Houston called his father to discuss all of the things they wanted to do for young people. Father and son decided that day to figure out the right way to give back all that God had blessed them with."

"How do we give back while passing on all of the life lessons I've learned from you, dad?" Allan asked his father.

They began to build the framework for a sustainable non-profit organization that had legs. They talked about developing and hosting basketball camps that would bring fathers and mentors in to learn the fundamentals that he grew up learning. But Houston and Coach Wade wanted to take it a step further. They decided to build a curriculum to teach fathers how to speak to their wives, how to discipline their children, how to teach, how to love, and how to talk to their kids about sex. Houston decided to bring all of these elements together in an environment where the fathers could have fun doing drills and participating in contests together.

After the first successful year, the program began to grow and attract the attention of influential executives who shared Houston's passion for improving the lives of fathers and sons. Three years later, an executive from Morgan Stanley participated in the program and expressed how much he loved coming to the camp. He asked Houston to meet with him to discuss the future of the program and how he might bring others to the table to help support Houston and his team's efforts. A result of the meeting was the opportunity for Houston to engage the National Foundation of Teaching Entrepreneurship (NFTE). With NFTE, Houston, his advisors, and staff developed a curriculum that would train eighteen- through twenty-five-year-olds on how to start their own business, and the self-sustainable model of training, equipping fathers, and mentoring was born. Houston understands and readily shares that no matter what they do or how many programs they successfully create, they are building a ministry. "We always want to make sure that we're showing God's heart through all of it and pointing them to Christ," Allan shares.

Wade is active with the Father Knows Best Program, a fatherhood mentoring and family restoration program. Father Knows Best came about when Houston and his dad were thinking about what to name the program. "We wanted the mentors as well as the fathers who would participate to know that we're not perfect as men or as fathers but there is a Heavenly Father who is available and is the father to us all. That's why we named it Father Knows Best Basketball," Allan explains. Wade is present and engaged in every one of the major launches, and it means the world to Houston to work side by side with his father—his de facto wingman—as they give back and uplift future generations and fathers who need and deserve all the support the world has to offer.

Dr. Thurman E. Hunt, MD

Anesthesiologist

"My father helped me navigate through life and allowed me to make mistakes on my own—something that I think is important."

Thurman E. Hunt, MD is the chair of Anesthesiology at Alameda County Medical Center in Oakland, California. Dr. Hunt graduated from the Stanford University School of Medicine in 1988 with research honors in psychiatry and immunology. He has led an extraordinary life as an anesthesiologist for more than twenty years due in part to the lessons he learned from his father, Delbert Wesley Hunt, Sr.

Delbert, born in 1926, dedicated much of his life to the fight for civil rights and equality for people of color. His dedication to providing a voice and fighting for fair and equal treatment for the underserved helped ignite his son's passion for treating those in need of medical care. Delbert founded the Detroit office for the Equal Employment Opportunity Commission and prior to that worked for the Civil Rights Commission as a private investigator. As a father and mentor, Delbert's passion for service to others was palpable. He was short on words but long on teaching invaluable lessons that encouraged his sons to develop a solid work ethic and pursue their dreams.

Delbert and his longtime love, Jean, married in 1956, and had two sons, Delbert Jr., born in 1957 and Thurman, born in 1960. Theirs was a working class family living in Detroit, Michigan. Hunt recalls one time when he got all A's on his report card and came home to proudly show his father how well he had done. His father just looked at the report card and smiled. He asked his son, "But did you learn anything?" Hunt thought that made an interesting statement about his father's perspective on learning. "You know, a lot of times people are really good at being students and getting good grades, but they don't know how to become life-long, independent learners and they want to focus only on the grade and content." Hunt recalls that his father's primary goal was to foster in his children the desire to get good grades not because of what he thought but because it was something they wanted to achieve. For Delbert, this intrinsic desire to succeed was most important. He never paid for grades or rewarded his sons with tangible things. Instead, he wanted his sons to motivate themselves until they got to the point that good grades meant nothing to them unless it came from within.

Hunt doesn't recall experiencing any real hardships as a child. "If it was going on they did a good job at protecting me from all of those things and that was probably choreographed," he says. "I think my parents did a good job of shielding me from tough times by managing my environment. They did that very well." Hunt believes, and many fathers would agree, that when children get a certain age, their peers have a tremendous amount of influence in their lives, even though parents may not like it. In retrospect, he feels that his father did a very good job of making sure he knew all of his friends and monitored his comings and goings very closely. His father made a conscious effort to redirect his son when necessary.

Hunt describes his father, who passed away in 2003, as a very serious man. Interestingly, his dad often made jokes and most people who came in contact with him found him to be fun loving. He would tell his sons that he was their father, not their friend and he never hesitated to draw the line, telling them the way life was, not the way life should be. His father didn't rule with an iron fist, but Hunt knew not to cross his dad. He recalls pushing the envelope a little more than his brother because he was a little bit more daring but thankfully, he didn't give his father much reason to discipline him. Hunt and his brother fought with each other around the house, but once they were outside of the house with their friends, they were family and knew how to behave themselves. His brother tells a story of someone picking on him. Their father caught wind of this and made sure that no matter what happened, his oldest son would take up for his younger brother and settle the issue later. To Delbert, their family bond was more important than anything and they always, always needed to stick up for one another.

Delbert and Jean considered themselves a team when it came to raising their two sons. They sent a unified message to illustrate to their children the importance of working together and speaking with one voice. Delbert was the breadwinner of the home and he was home a great deal in the evenings and on the weekends. Though his dad often showed his serious side, there was also a warmth about him, and he was present at everything his sons participated in—from school activities to Little League baseball games.

Hunt recalls that everyone had responsibilities in the Hunt home including the children. He remembers his mother telling him that if he ever did something that landed him in jail, she would only come visit him once. Hunt knows without question that his parents loved and cared about him, but he also knew that they had rules that he had to follow.

The family spent time together attending church services at different times in Hunt's life, and he grew up in Sunday school. He wouldn't say necessarily that his father was deeply religious, but he *was* deeply spiritual. Hunt considered his father a good financial steward. In fact, both of his parents encouraged him to save. He remembers his father taking him down to the bank to open a savings account just as soon as he was old enough to write his own name.

Hunt remembers a time in 1967 right after the Detroit riots when the family moved from the Russell Woods neighborhood to what is now referred to as the University District. He was just seven years old, and his brother was ten. The boys were students at Winterhalter Elementary School, just five miles away from their new home in the University District, and their mother wanted them to finish out the school year with minimal disruption. One day Jean took the boys on a city bus and showed them how to pay the bus fare and where to get on the bus to go directly to school. The next day, Hunt and his big brother got on the bus and went to school as they were told. Thinking of just how much times have changed, he recently asked his mother what possessed her to put her two small children on a public bus to make their way to school each day, particularly with so much civil unrest going on in Detroit at that time. She matter-of-factly told him, they were working-class people, and they had to learn to be self-sufficient. "That was it," Thurman says. "It was done and we never had an issue. I knew I had to behave, go to school and do what I needed to do."

When Hunt was twelve years old, he desperately wanted a ten-speed bike. His father did not buy him the bike, and this deeply disappointed him. In retrospect, he believes his dad didn't buy the bike because he was trying to teach him a sense of independence and instill in him the drive to go after the things he wanted in life. His father told him to take his own money and go out and buy the bike, and that's exactly what he did. He used the money he earned from his paper route and the small business he started with a friend, Stanley, shoveling snow, cutting grass, running errands, and cleaning windows to purchase the bike himself for $98.80. He was immensely proud, and from this experience he learned that if he wanted something bad enough, with hard work and careful planning, he had the ability to go out and get it for himself.

Hunt's parents never gave him any money for allowance or anything, really. Because there were things that he wanted to buy, like a ten-speed bike, he was motivated to be industrious and start his own business. In junior high school, he and his buddy, Stanley, opened a stand called "Sister Kay's Steak and Take." Essentially they started a little "restaurant" making steak hoagies and all kinds of sandwiches and snacks. In high school, Hunt worked in the Federals Department Store as a stock boy. Later, he got a job that he really liked filling prescriptions at Band Drugs, the neighborhood pharmacy. This was Hunt's official foray into medicine. The pharmacist bought him a subscription to *Scientific American.* He couldn't fully understand the articles, but his curiosity about medicine was piqued. He started reading what he could in *Scientific American* and asking questions about the medical field.

For all intents and purposes, as he got older his father let him do things he wanted to do. His brother went to Bishop Borgess, the Catholic School High School his parents wanted him to attend. Three years later when it was time for Hunt to go to high school he decided on his own that he would go to Cass Technical High School and that there would be no family meeting to discuss his decision. His parents weren't involved at all in major education-related decisions like which colleges he would apply to. He remembers having a conversation with his father and mother about college, and they never told Hunt that he definitely had to go to college. "They basically told me, 'We live here, and we are a working family so either you get a job or you go to college,'" Thurman says. He never went on a college tour to decide which college campus he liked best or which type of institution would best fit his needs academically or socially.

Essentially, he got a book about various colleges and universities and looked at materials from the schools that sent him information.

After applying to and being accepted to several large universities, he accepted the offer to attend the University of Michigan. At that time, he never considered how he would pay for college. When he sat down with his parents to discuss enrolling in and paying for his secondary education, his father told him they would do what they could. "I knew that was a bad sign," Thurman says. "So I said I would go to the University of Michigan and work in the summertime to pay for it. What I didn't have I could take out loans for." The summer before his freshman year, Hunt was offered a full ride scholarship because he worked for Detroit Edison in the summers and they offered scholarships to deserving students entering the through the Detroit Area Pre-College Engineering Program (DAPCEP). As he matriculated, Hunt became a resident advisor in his dormitory, which paid for his room and board, and he earned additional money with his college friend, George Crawford, by way of a soda concession in their dormitory. Between the two, he had the money to pay his college tuition and decided to give up his engineering scholarship and focus on premed.

Hunt graduated from Michigan with a degree in cellular and molecular biology in 1982. His parents were proud that after graduating from the University of Michigan, he decided to go to medical school. He even remembers telling his mother of his desire to become a doctor. "Are you sure you want to do that?" his mother asked. She was concerned that medicine didn't necessarily fit Hunt's personality and thought engineering was a better fit for him. Nonetheless, both his father and mother supported his decision to go to medical school and he knew they were happy that he was accomplishing the goals he set for himself.

After graduating from Stanford University School of Medicine in 1988, Hunt completed his internship and finished his residency at the University of Medicine and Dentistry of New Jersey. He spent five years in New Jersey while his wife, Stacey, also a physician, completed her training. Thurman and Stacey then moved back to the Midwest for three years when he accepted a position as the chair of anesthesiology at Hurley Medical Center in Flint, Michigan. He had an opportunity to return to California to practice at Alameda County Medical Center and has been there for over eleven years. Hunt and Stacey have been married for over twenty years. They have two children, Jordan and Morgan.

Throughout his life and his medical career, Hunt's dad encouraged him to do a lot of self-exploration. Hunt recalls his father telling him to always be truthful with himself. "That rings true to me today," Thurman says. "I try to be honest with myself, and I try to pay attention to the things that motivate me. I think a lot about my father's words."

Hunt tries to instill in his children some of the same values his father instilled in him and his older brother, but he doesn't go about it the same way. The fundamental values he is passing on to his son and daughter include independence and simply put, being good and responsible people. "It was something that I think we just got growing up," Thurman says. "But the way people grow up now, so fast and with so much information coming at them, they are growing up in the age of the Internet. They see and think quicker because they are so intelligent, and this has a tendency to make them grow up fast so it's hard to instill in them the kind of work ethic we learned." Still, Hunt teaches his children that they must work at something they love a little bit every day over a long period of time in order to have a greater sense of discipline. He tries to teach Jordan and Morgan, both piano players, that they must have a sense of a mastery over something and the importance of working hard to accomplish their goals.

Hunt recalls that his fondest memory of his father was spending time with his father at the beach collecting seashells and just playing catch. His dad loved baseball and in hindsight, Hunt understands why his father encouraged him and his brother to play Little League baseball. "I believe he thought that if he had to suffer through all of the practices and everything he might as well pick a sport that he liked," Thurman says, laughing.

The most important thing Hunt wants the world to know about his father is that he dealt with both of his sons evenly and gave them what they needed individually. His father worked with each of his sons to bring out their strengths and to the extent possible, mitigate their weaknesses. His father helped them navigate through life allowing them to make mistakes on their own.

Major General Marcia M. Anderson

United States Army Reserve
Two-Star General

"My father came of age when the world was changing but not fast enough to appreciate his talents, and yet he still made the most of his life... I am incredibly proud that he refused to let adversity or discrimination discourage or define him."

The most extraordinary leaders are sometimes the unassuming ones who lead with intellect and instinct instead of ego. Major General Marcia M. Anderson is exactly that type of leader who has brought a quiet sense of dignity and discernment to an illustrious thirty-three-year military career. On September 29, 2011, she became the first African American woman awarded a second star as a general in the United States Army, making her one of the most powerful women in the armed forces. According to Anderson, it was a day black soldiers who have served our country could never have imagined. It was a day her father, Rudolph Mahan, will never forget.

Upon witnessing his daughter's promotion, Rudolph, now in his mid-80s, began to reflect on his own military career and has talked with his daughter about his unfulfilled dreams of flying bombers in the military. Rudolph served in the United States Air Force during the Korean War just a few years after the armed forces were integrated in 1948, but it would be many years before soldiers of color would receive the same opportunities as their white counterparts. During his time in the Air Force, Rudolph never got to fly bombers. Instead, he worked as a supply clerk and a truck driver. His dreams, however, have lived on through his daughter's celebrated military career. Nothing could have made him prouder than to witness her success, which Anderson says is for "people like her dad who had dreams deferred." Today, Anderson accepts her position as a two star general in the United States Army Reserve with equal parts humility and strategy. Though she has experienced unparalleled success, she has never once lost sight of what her father went through to make her career possible.

Her father was born in Beloit, Wisconsin. Rudolph graduated from Beloit Memorial High School, the only high school in Beloit at the time. The school was integrated by default simply because there were no separate schools or facilities for people of color. On one occasion, Rudolph and a few of his high school friends decided it would be fun to "borrow" a car to take on a joyride out of the state. The boys wanted to join the military but because none of their parents would allow them, they decided to find a location in another town to enlist. They got as far as Kansas when the police pulled them over in this car that didn't belong to any of them. Once the police officers found out where the young black males were from, their plot was foiled. The officers contacted their parents and Rudolph and his friends were transported back home to Wisconsin. Anderson contends that her father has told this story so many times over the years that it has officially taken on a life of its own. Several years after the joyride, Rudolph managed to enlist in the military and after his years of service ended, he returned to Wisconsin and worked in a local hotel, followed by a job at the Fairbanks Morse Corporation and later at the Beloit Corporation.

Anderson's parents divorced and her mother, Floye Mahan, moved the two children to East St. Louis, where she'd grown up. Anderson was entering second grade. Despite their divorce, Rudolph and Floye maintained a good relationship and Anderson appreciates that her mother never had a disparaging word to say about her father. She and her father always exchanged cards and letters, and talked on the phone regularly. At the close of each school year, she and her younger brother traveled to Wisconsin to spend summers with their dad. He would also travel to East St. Louis to visit them on occasion. The time they spent together going out to see a movie or a children's show always felt special to Anderson, and she has never taken it for granted. She has a lot of friends who never knew their fathers and recognized early in life that the father-daughter relationship is a blessing.

Anderson recalls that her mother would let her dad know whenever she did something good in school or received an award.

When Rudolph learned of the good news he would send his daughter a small gift or a card and five dollars, which seemed like a lot of money to a young girl. In recent years, Rudolph began sending her birthday cards with coins taped inside to represent the number of years of her life. For her last birthday, she received a card with fifty-four cents taped inside. She loves her father's thoughtfulness and keeps every single card he has sent over the years.

Anderson understood her father's expectations even when he didn't articulate them, and she never wanted to fail him. Even though he didn't spell out specific goals that she must meet regarding education, she just felt in her head and her heart that she wanted him to be proud of her. After high school, Anderson attended Creighton University in Omaha, Nebraska, where she worked her way through school doing work-study jobs to help pay for her education. She also received grants and small scholarships to fill the financial gaps. To fulfill a science requirement, she decided to sign up for what she later found out was an Army ROTC class that would ultimately change the course of her life.

The class gave Anderson her first exposure to the United States military and she was required at the end of the semester to decide whether or not she had an interest in staying with the ROTC program. She enjoyed the class and decided to continue especially when she learned that upon graduation she would be commissioned as a Second Lieutenant with the option of going into active duty or the Army Reserve. Anderson chose to go into the Army Reserve because she didn't know anyone doing active duty and wasn't willing to make such a big commitment at that point. The process required her to perform reserve duty on a part-time basis while maintaining her civilian employment. Anderson grew from the experience of being in the reserves while maintaining her life as a civilian. She began to think there was something special about pursuing a military career that just might pique her interest long term, but she knew she wanted to pursue a law degree first.

After graduating from Rutgers School of Law, Anderson clerked for a state judge, followed by working for the federal court in New York City. The young lawyer decided that she needed to experience private practice, so she joined a firm in New Jersey doing litigation, an area of the law she didn't like. Anderson then went in-house for a major utility company as corporate counsel working on environmental and employment law matters. She enjoyed practicing law but felt that something was missing. Because she was committed to public service, she went back into the federal court system and has been there ever since.

Since her promotion in 2011, her father no longer refers to her as Marcia. He calls her "General," which she finds funny. When she found out she'd been nominated, she first called her husband Amos, and then her dad. Her father answered the phone and Anderson calmly said to him, "Look, I have just been nominated, but it's not confirmed yet, so it's not a done deal. Anything can happen, but I wanted you to know." She knew there was the nomination process followed by a US Senate confirmation, so she didn't want her father to get too excited just yet. Rudolph expressed his joy and said, "Ok, I got it." He agreed not to talk to anyone about the potential promotion. Twenty minutes later, Anderson called her father again. Her stepmother answered the phone and explained that her father, who only has a small fringe of hair left on his nearly bald head, was off to the barbershop. She knew immediately what happened. Her dad was bursting at the seams and went to share the news with all of his friends at the local barbershop. "He was just really excited and proud of me and he couldn't contain himself," Anderson explained. His proudest moment is when he tells people that she is his daughter. In her opinion, this doesn't diminish him in any way at all. "It clearly says that he did okay because I had her," explains Marcia.

Anderson never aspired to be a two-star general. She joined the military completely on a fluke after randomly choosing the Army ROTC class in college to fulfill her science credit. She has, however, enjoyed her ever-changing role as she has climbed the ranks in the Army Reserve. She looked up and ten years had passed. She then thought that at the twenty-year mark in the military she would make Lieutenant Colonel, which would allow her to command and serve as Senior Staff Officer. With each promotion, people began to encourage her and she established relationships with special mentors. Anderson acknowledges that as she continues to navigate the waters of a successful career as the first African American female major general, she faces extreme pressure. Nevertheless, she is determined to enjoy the fruits of her labor and embrace the good and the bad. The fact that she is an Army Reserve general with duty at the Pentagon motivates a lot of people. She realizes, however, that this historical accomplishment is not about her. It is about the next generation. "I act with integrity and I make sure I follow the regulations," Marcia says. "I try to model the right way to do business and a lot of that is from my dad who told me that I have been given this opportunity and should not squander it. Again, it's not about me."

Although Rudolph has never been much of a talker, today it doesn't take much to get him going. He has begun to engage in political discourse and recently went as far as writing a letter to the editor of the Beloit newspaper about Medicare and Medicare costs—something completely uncharacteristic of him. The editorial staff decided to publish the letter and her dad proudly sent Anderson the clipping from the newspaper. She was pleased that he took such a bold stance on an issue he cared about because this is one of those things she never really expected her father to do.

Her dad retired many years ago, but in his second "career" he mentors children. He loves working with the kids at Merrill Elementary School, where Anderson attended kindergarten. Her dad helps serve the kids breakfast, a mid-day snack, and lunch. He talks with Anderson often about the kids and shares that many don't have fathers or grandfathers in their lives. Some of the children come to school at the beginning of the school year without being taught to respect their elders, but by the first week, they have learned to call him Mr. Mahan. And as they walk down the streets of Beloit, if they see their favorite school mentor, they excitedly point him out to their parents, yelling, "That's Mr. Mahan. He works at my school!"

Rudolph has also become very involved in his church, "To the point now we have to say a prayer at a meal, and it can go on for awhile," Marcia says, laughing. "I started calling him reverend." Her father wasn't nearly as involved as a younger man, but as he got older being involved in church became important to him. Today, he participates in church activities, and he is a part of a men's choir who sings at various community events.

Anderson respects the fact her father has discovered new interests later in life. Likewise, he respects his daughter's sense of adventure and her ability to try new things. A few years ago, Anderson called her dad and told him she was at Fort Benning Infantry School participating in a parachute-training course. Her father said, "You're in jump school?" He told her when he was in the Air Force they had to do an orientation parachute jump that didn't qualify them for anything, but in basic training they had to jump out of an airplane. Rudolph didn't like the experience and naturally felt concerned that his daughter was jumping voluntarily. He made her promise to call him when the jump course was over. Anderson obliged. Her father was relieved that she landed safely, and although he respects her fearlessness, he still couldn't believe she voluntarily jumped out of an airplane.

Anderson sometimes hears her father's voice in her head when taking on new challenges or dealing with difficult work issues. "It goes beyond the old adage, 'Treat others the way you would like to be treated,' Marcia says. "I always try to treat people with respect, not assuming that because I have all of these degrees or that having degrees makes me the smartest person in the room, but because I learned how to treat people from my father." There have been times in her military career when she has faced men who feel that women are taking up a space that a man should have. Taking a page from her father's playbook, Anderson carefully handles these negative situations by speaking her mind without engaging in a full-on confrontation and exceeding everyone's expectations—all life lessons from her father.

The most significant life lesson Anderson has learned from her father is essentially how he has handled disappointment in his life and how he resolved to do the best he can with the opportunities he has been given. She took notes on how he gracefully handled losing his pension and medical benefits when the company he retired from became insolvent and filed for bankruptcy. She reflects on how he didn't get depressed about it and he didn't "rail against the machine." He simply has accepted those types of adversities, developed a new plan, and executed on it.

Today, Anderson and her father take as many opportunities as they can to enjoy their relationship. Rudolph has taken up golf, and they have played together, though she would argue it's probably dangerous to other golfers when the father-daughter duo is on a golf course together. Still, they enjoy walking the course together as they golf. She looks at it as an opportunity to talk about things with her father. They also go to his favorite restaurant where they sit, order his regular steak meal, and talk. Sometimes it's just the two of them laughing and sharing stories or just sitting quietly together.

The most important thing Major General Anderson wants the world to know about her father is that he came of age when the world was changing but not fast enough to appreciate his talents. Yet, he still made the most of his life and didn't let adversity or discrimination discourage him. Her father figured out ways to take care of his family. He did what he needed to do and he never let discrimination of any kind become a barrier to living a fulfilled life.

Tracy Maitland

Wall Street Investment Manager

"My father dedicated his life to helping all types of people that needed medical care and he never turned anybody away. People have come to me on many occasions and said, 'Your father saved my life.'"

Native New Yorker and extraordinary investment manager Tracy Maitland has long been considered one of the biggest names on Wall Street throughout his more than twenty years as a leader in the financial industry. Maitland is president and chief investment officer of Advent Capital Management, a multi-billion dollar diversified investment firm specializing in convertible, high yield, and equity strategies. He started his illustrious career with Merrill Lynch where he spent thirteen years advising institutions on investing in convertibles, fixed income, and equities. Featured on Forbes list of 20 Wealthiest Blacks in America in 2009, Maitland is literally and figuratively giving the good ol' boys on Wall Street a run for their money. Much of his drive and inspiration come from none other than his father, Dr. Leo C. Maitland, who showed Maitland what success looked like from the time he was old enough to read the *Wall Street Journal*. Dr. Maitland was a prominent New York surgeon known to many as the "doctor to the stars." Considered outspoken and thoughtful, Dr. Maitland defined in his own distinct way what it meant to be an excellent physician and an extraordinary man.

Leo Maitland, born in 1928, was raised in New York with his sister Sylvia by very strict parents. He graduated from City College of New York and went to medical school at Meharry Medical College in Nashville, Tennessee. He was a captain in the United States Air Force only ten years after President Truman integrated the military in 1948. While serving, Dr. Maitland performed over 2000 operations.

He met and married Carolyn Swann, who was also raised in New York. After graduating from Syracuse University, Carolyn earned an MFA and a doctorate in education from Teacher's College, Columbia University. Leo and Carolyn had three children, Leo E., Tracy, and Anne, all four years apart. Today, Carolyn is a celebrated printmaker and watercolor artist, and has served as the president of the National Council for African American Artists. Maitland always appreciated that he and his siblings were exposed to culture and the arts through their mother's passion but also through exposure to their father's impressive patients and close friends.

Dr. Maitland's altruistic commitment to caring for the community is something Maitland witnessed most of his young life. The celebrated physician built a thriving private practice in Harlem, which he later moved to New York's Upper West Side. He also worked at several New York hospitals including New York University and Sydenham Hospital, where he was chairman and associate director for the surgery department. Maitland's father was an extraordinarily successful doctor in an era when doctors were thought of as being very prestigious, particularly in the African American community. Dr. Maitland was considered an institution in the neighborhood where he established his thriving private practice and was well known throughout New York City. Included amongst his well-to-do patients and friends in the arts and entertainment fields were Diahann Carroll, Geoffrey Holder, Quincy Troupe, Maya Angelou and Miles Davis, to name but a few. In fact, the Maitland family grew close to Miles Davis and would spend time with him in his Manhattan home. In her autobiography, *Gather Together In My Name*, Maya Angelou mentioned Dr. Maitland as one of her "other real brothers who encouraged me to be bodacious enough to invent my own daily life."

In 1958 Dr. Maitland, then a surgical resident, was on the medical team at Harlem Hospital that operated on Dr. Martin Luther King Jr. after he was stabbed in the chest at a Harlem book signing. He and Dr. King later became friends and after Dr. Maitland died in 1992, Maitland found books belonging to his father that were authored by Dr. King. In them, he discovered that Dr. King had written personal notes to his father. While Dr. Maitland treasured his friendships with national figures and prominent local leaders and politicians, his work extended far beyond caring for individuals with larger than life resumes and images. He derived a great deal of satisfaction from treating his day-to-day patients, including patients who could not afford to pay.

Maitland recalls that his father was always interested in medicine. Most members of the Maitland family also trained and worked in the medical field, which according to Maitland makes him the black sheep of the family. His uncle was also a surgeon, his maternal grandmother was a nurse, and his sister is a practicing physician. As a child, Maitland, who never liked blood or diseases, accompanied his dad on his hospital rounds to see patients when he was young. For the life of him, he couldn't figure out what was so interesting or intriguing about medicine and found that going on rounds with his dad was particularly helpful because it helped him figure out what he did *not* want to be when he grew up. This early exposure to hospitals and sick people made his decision to go into a profession that had nothing to do with medicine quite simple.

However, seeing his father as a successful physician and business owner left an indelible mark on a young man who aspired to build wealth and one day become financially independent just like his dad. Though he chose a different professional path, he understood at an early age that his father provided a legacy of greatness and that he too would one day be extraordinary in his own right.

All three of the Maitland children had very different relationships with their father and yet, they all loved him dearly. While Maitland and his father got along great, the relationship between his brother and father was very different. "My brother,

Leo, is artistic and creative," Tracy explains. "He ended up earning a Master's degree from Columbia, so he was certainly driven." Presently Leo is a teacher and a musician living in Spain who trained under famed South African trumpeter and composer, Hugh Masekela. Anne, the youngest of the Maitland children, was always driven from the time she was a young girl. She was a straight-A student and a track star, earning a spot on Yale University's track team as a sprinter. After receiving her Bachelor's degree from Yale, Anne, with a great deal of guidance from her father, decided to enter a joint MD, PhD program at the University of Pennsylvania. She became the very first African American to graduate from the program. According to Maitland, his sister was "definitely all about people and medicine." Today, Anne is assistant professor at the Icahn School of Medicine at Mount Sinai in the Clinical Immunology Division of the Medicine Department.

None of the Maitland kids would consider their father a harsh disciplinarian. Maitland remembers his dad as a mellow guy, but when he meant business, they knew it. From Maitland's perspective, his father's version of discipline was essentially improvising and making adjustments for things that he saw that his son needed to do better. He was always very supportive, constantly analyzing what was going on in Tracy's life. "My father would think about what he perceived as a weakness for me and would try to compensate for it, like when he hired tutors for me," Tracy explained. "I think he just wanted me to do well." As many loving, present fathers do,

Dr. Maitland provided his son with all of the assistance he could possibly need, even when Maitland didn't feel he needed it. Dr. Maitland decided one year that his youngest son needed to speak a language so he sent him to Canada for a summer during his high school years to learn French. As a child Maitland was motivated because he wanted to do well in school and in life, and his father knew that. His father was successful and just being around him made Maitland want to be successful too. "Standing six foot four, he just had this presence, this aura," Tracy says. "I don't know if you've ever been around Bill Clinton, but like Bill Clinton, my dad just kind of had that energy people would gravitate to."

Maitland's parents separated when he was in his early teens, but their separation never diminished the love they shared for all three of their children, and it showed in myriad ways. He began to realize, as he got older that his mother and father were just very different people. He doesn't recall any negative experiences related to his parents' relationship because they equally respected their positions as nurturers and providers, and above all they remained friends. Despite their separation, they made it a priority to celebrate holidays and birthdays together as a family. Most important, his relationship with his dad didn't change. He would go back and forth between his father's home and his mother's home. He found the transition interesting in some ways because he grew up in the Bronx, and, later, his father moved to Manhattan, which to Maitland seemed to be the new, exciting place to be. His dad was in the mix of so many interesting people.

Dr. Maitland indirectly had an impact on his son's decision to go into finance. Because he saw his dad build his practice with great success, it sparked Maitland's interest in entrepreneurship and it became clear to the future Wall Street power broker that he too wanted to be in control of his own destiny. This was one of the most important lessons his father taught him and he watched, listened, and learned from his father throughout middle school, high school, and college. Both of his parents believed strongly in establishing a good educational foundation for their kids. They sent young Tracy to Barnard, an exclusive private school in Riverdale in the Bronx that later was merged into The Horace Mann School.

Maitland recalls being one of the only African American kids in his class for many years. All of his friends outside of Barnard attended public school and because Maitland felt he was missing out on the public school experience with his friends, he made a strong case to his parents to change schools. His parents finally relented and transferred him to public school where he was considered an advanced student. He attended the public school with his friends for only two weeks. "I got there, and the other black kids were trying to beat up the white kids, the white kids were trying to beat up the black kids, and it was just chaos," Tracy says. "Coming from a mellow private school, I felt that it was a crazy environment, and I knew that wasn't going to work for me.'" Maitland remembers the students being asked about what their parents did for a living. When it was his turn, he told the class his father was a surgeon and his mother was a teacher. No one believed him, including his teacher. He knew right then and there it was time for him to go.

His parents took him out of public school immediately and enrolled him in an all black school called Our Saviour Lutheran. Going from an all white school to an all black school helped Maitland become well rounded. The experience gave him confidence, taught him how to communicate with people from different backgrounds, and made him comfortable in his own skin. According to Maitland, he learned to "play both sides of the fence." Admittedly, the black school provided a good education, but it didn't have the academic rigor that he experienced at Barnard. Thus, being near the top of the class and doing well academically came easy to him. Maitland found himself "skating along for the most part and having a good time." He recalls that Our Saviour Lutheran had a great basketball team, but all of the cool people and the popular students were in the choir. "That made my experience at Lutheran really interesting and fun," says Tracy. His father, however, felt that he wasn't applying himself and feared that he wouldn't get into a great college, so he pulled his son out of Our Saviour Lutheran during his senior year and enrolled him in The New Lincoln School, a private school in Manhattan where some of the kids were already starting to read the *Wall Street Journal.*

Maitland respected his father's decision to provide him with the best education possible. He believed there was an upside to attending three different schools prior to attending college—he developed a keen ability to adapt to a variety of situations. He learned to be a leader and embraced change with an open mind. In addition to the lessons he learned at home, his educational experiences—both inside and outside of the classroom—helped him develop exemplary social skills and shaped his values. "Going to these schools and handling these situations taught me to deal with lots of different types of people whether they lived in the projects or on Park Avenue," Tracy says. He graduated from The New Lincoln School and went on to Columbia University where he earned a Bachelor's degree in economics.

Most people approach college as the opportunity to get away from their parents in order to have their own lives, but because Maitland and his father were good friends, he didn't feel that way at all. Maitland loved attending college in New York. He understood that Columbia University was an Ivy League school, and he came to the conclusion that there was no need to go anywhere else. Essentially, Maitland had the best of both worlds and would do it again in a heartbeat. Between having access to his father's influential friends and being in the epicenter of the financial world, he got a great deal of exposure to an industry that he would later dominate. In the summers, he interned at a couple of investment firms where he began to have a true understanding of Wall Street.

Many of the people in his father's life became mentors to Maitland. They allowed him to visit their offices, giving him an up close and personal view of how they conducted business and how they became successful. All Maitland had to do was ask and doors were opened for him because his father was greatly admired and respected. "If it wasn't for that I wouldn't have been on Wall Street," Tracy admits. Conversely, there were people in his life that tried to discourage him from pursuing a career in finance. "I remember going to see this black guy on Wall Street who agreed to meet with me," he says. "When I sat down with him he says, 'I don't know why you want to come to Wall Street. Why don't you go work for Proctor and Gamble or something?'" Maitland surmised that happened for two reasons: One, he wanted to be the only black executive at this particular firm because if Maitland came there and did well, it would make him look bad; and two, if Maitland screwed up, it would make him look bad. Being able to understand where he was coming from and not take it personally was a function of Maitland's upbringing. It was also a function of being with his father, who surrounded himself with a lot of strong and successful people.

As the young finance executive's career took off and he became increasingly successful, his father developed a keen interest in Wall Street. Dr. Maitland bought a subscription to the *Wall Street Journal* so he could keep up with what was happening on Wall Street, and father and son would converse about finance all the time. Though medicine was his father's first love, Maitland watched with joy how his father began to take a real interest in the world of finance.

Dr. Maitland had to have the latest gadgets and sports cars and Maitland knows beyond a shadow of a doubt that his dad's appreciation for gadgets and the latest "toys" rubbed off on him. His father was a connoisseur of the finer things—from high fidelity audio to fine wines, from exquisite cuisine to literature. He was well read and always had interesting things to talk about or opinions about relevant and not-so-relevant issues, all of which helped Maitland "elevate." All through his life, Dr. Maitland maintained a curiosity and a love for learning. "If you go to a doctor, you want somebody that's always curious about the latest in technology and the latest medical advances," says Tracy.

As a practicing physician and surgeon, Dr. Maitland spent long hours building his practice and treating patients. As a result, he didn't have a lot of free time and did not spend an inordinate amount of time with his children. As Maitland got older, father and son spent a lot more quality time together, often with friends. Dr. Maitland loved to host dinner parties at his house, always finding a reason to entertain. "If it was time for the Kentucky Derby, there would be a Kentucky Derby dinner party at his house," Tracy recalls. "He came up with whatever excuse he could find to have a social event. That's how much he loved to entertain and spend time with friends." He and his dad also spent a lot of time hanging out in Manhattan together. Dr. Maitland was extremely New York City-centric and helped Maitland appreciate that New York is where you really want to be for a variety of reasons. Maitland had to drag his dad out of New York to get him to see other places. In the mid 80s, Maitland announced to his family that he was moving to Detroit for work. His father's response: "What? Where is that?" Dr. Maitland pointed out to his son that millions of people leave small towns around the world to come to New York and asked him why he would ever want to leave New York and go to some "little town." To this day, Maitland can't recall if his father ever came to visit him in the three years he lived in the Midwest.

As a leading philanthropist and the founder of Advent Capital, Maitland is deeply tied into New York's philanthropic community and sits on several boards including The American Society for the Prevention of Cruelty of Animals, the Studio Museum of Harlem, Columbia University Board of Visitors, the Apollo Theater and the Managed Fund Association (MFA), which caters to the hedge fund industry. He also serves as chairman of the board of Advent Capital Management, a publicly traded mutual fund traded on the New York Stock Exchange. He approaches his work at Advent Capital and his board duties with the same fervor and passion that his father approached his life's work as a physician. Maitland is keenly aware that he cannot keep up this pace forever and will eventually decrease at least some of his civic involvement. Until then, he will continue to give of his time, talent, and financial resources to benefit others.

Dr. Maitland would most certainly be proud of the extraordinary man Maitland has become. Maitland misses his father and friend, but recognizes that his dad lived an extraordinary life. He recalls that when his father died, literally thousands of people attended his funeral at the oldest African American

Episcopal Church in Harlem, St. Philip's Church, where Dr. Maitland served as an acolyte decades prior. He impacted the lives of so many—from politicians to people in the arts to every day citizens of New York. At his funeral, countless people came up to Maitland and his siblings to share how their father "saved my life" and to express how much he meant to the community. Maitland never heard anyone say a bad thing about his dad.

His father dedicated his life to helping people and he never turned anyone away. Leo C. Maitland served as a fine example of manhood, and Maitland is especially proud of the many lessons his dad taught him that helped him become the man he is today.

Juana Wooldridge

Author and Radio Personality

"My dad has always taken care of his family. He has always been a shining example of a resilient African American father."

Life isn't always sweet, especially when society tries to sell the image of the idealistic family. We've all seen it—the utopian vision of family life complete with two successful, doting parents and a brood of smart, well-adjusted children. This is often a fairy tale, and it certainly isn't one that describes most American families.

In order to be truthful and balanced, we must introduce the narrative of the Black family that illustrates victory over pain and triumph over true adversity. These are often the stories that take our breath away and make us reflect on what it means to grow when life brings us to our knees. These stories provide examples of strength and fortitude that come along at the right time. Just as we relish lessons that glorify family life and make us feel good about our place in the world, it is equally important to heed the lessons that sting a bit and make us a little uncomfortable.

Juana Patricia Wooldridge wears several titles at this stage in her life, including single mother, author, student, blogger, and motivational speaker. She is also the creator of The Heart of the World Skincare and a celebrated radio personality, hosting weekly shows that cover sports, entertainment, politics, faith and spirituality, and relationships. She uplifts and inspires the masses with lessons she has learned that have made her wiser and more resilient than she ever thought possible.

For Wooldridge, life hasn't always been sweet, and her road hasn't been smooth. Nevertheless, she tells all who will listen that she is blessed and highly favored. She has faced challenges that could easily take down the mightiest soul. But for all of the obstacles she has endured, there have been triumphant moments— moments of clarity and introspection, moments of forgiveness and understanding, moments that shook her to the core and forced her to redefine life on her own terms. She has, however, been steadfast in her belief in God and His ability to carry her through the darkest times. Wooldridge is a thirty-five-year-old rare beauty known to render men speechless when they lay eyes on her chiseled cheeks bones, flawless complexion, and dazzling brown eyes. Her physical beauty, however, pales in comparison to the beauty that lives inside her heart. While only God and genetics can be credited with her physical beauty, her internal beauty is due in large part to the bright lights in her life—her relationship with her five-year-old son, Blace, her father, David, and God.

Wooldridge learned to be a survivor from her father, David Wooldridge, Jr. Her dad helped her develop resilience and uplifted her when she didn't feel she had the strength to carry on.

Her journey is about a strong-willed, supportive father and his equally strong-willed, determined daughter whose triumphs in life are a reflection of her inner strength and her father's love. She has arrived at a place of acceptance and understanding about difficult personal choices she has made and casts no aspersions on her family for whom love springs eternal.

Wooldridge was born in Los Angeles to David and Stephanie Wooldridge. She was raised with one older sister, Karien, a younger brother, Malcolm, and a younger sister, Brandi. Her father, David, is the oldest of three sons born to David Sr. and Juana Natalie Wooldridge. During many of their father-daughter talks, David has shared accounts of his upbringing with his daughter. According to Wooldridge, her grandparents are wonderful human beings and well-respected members of their community who have nurtured, loved, and supported their three sons fiercely. They were, however, firm disciplinarians. David Sr., her grandfather, adopted a "spare the rod, spoil the child" position when it came to raising his boys, especially his oldest, David Jr. This heavy-handed approach to discipline is prevalent in many African American homes because parents feel that if they fail to teach their children important lessons on how to behave properly at home, they will learn these lessons in more destructive and damaging ways as they go out into the world to face racism and encounter people who do not have their best interest at heart. David never liked or agreed with the way his parents, particularly his father, disciplined him. The beatings troubled him profoundly, and he rebelled. He got involved with gangs and drugs and many of his friends landed in jail. He stayed in trouble and caused his parents a great deal of anxiety as he ran the streets of Los Angeles with the wrong crowd.

David attended Fairfax High School, where he was a star football player. He was handsome, charming, and smart enough to get people to do his homework for him. He was diagnosed with dyslexia, a condition for which his parents got him help and support, but at the time dyslexia was not widely understood or treated. As a result, David struggled. He received classroom help from coaches, teachers, and fellow students but this kind of *help* didn't do much good because he finished high school unable to read.

David met the beautiful, Stephanie Vest in 1973. They fell quickly for one another and dated only a few months before Stephanie became pregnant with their oldest child in 1974. They decided to get married when David was just seventeen years old. Stephanie was eighteen. They started a life together, but David had a dark cloud hanging over his head. His ability to provide for his family, especially as they had more healthy, beautiful children, was severely limited. He knew that in order to create better opportunities for himself and his family, he must learn to read. And that's exactly what he did, with a great deal of handholding and guidance from Stephanie. Eventually, the young husband and father received an exciting opportunity to play college football at Murray State University in Kentucky where he worked hard on the field and in the classroom. Though he faced self-imposed roadblocks early on, David was always intelligent and incredibly driven. With financial support from his parents, he worked through college and earned a Bachelor's degree in journalism. In 1982 he went to work with his father, David Sr., at Motorola in Chicago. David Sr. was corporate vice president and the first African American officer at Motorola. The two became legendary at the company, with the younger David eventually earning the coveted position of national sales manager of the intelligent vehicle highways systems strategic business unit. Though David and his father did not see eye to eye in his younger years, the father and son duo made a dynamic executive team. His appointment in 1990 at age thirty-four, to oversee the $1.2 million sales budget for the company's new user-friendly navigation technology, gave credence to Motorola's—and his father's—confidence in his abilities. During this time, David soared professionally and his life with his family benefited as well. Wooldridge feels that her father and mother had a true partnership. Her mother did not work outside of the home but carried the tremendous responsibility of raising their four children, supporting David in myriad of ways as he climbed the corporate ladder.

According to Wooldridge, her dad is a walking dictionary. Anyone who engages him in conversation or has the opportunity to work with him would be amazed that this articulate, intellectual man did not know how to read in high school. David has overcome many challenges and as an executive working alongside his father, he dealt with the subtle and not-so-subtle nuances of corporate racism and prejudice in an environment where the stakes are high for successful black executives.

Though their relationship was difficult when David was younger, the elder David continued to demonstrate his support in many ways. He also passed on a solid work ethic to David and his two brothers. Wooldridge is quick to share that the men in her family are considered *alpha males*. Her grandfather, a man who has always done exceptionally well and has broken barriers for other African American executives, taught all three of his sons to speak out and be tough in the face of adversity. He taught them to be willing to stand up and do the right thing, even if that meant pushing back in a constructive way. From him they learned that even rebellion has its place. This idea of questioning and rearing against authority when necessary had a profound impact on Wooldridge. She watched the men in her family closely as she grew up and she clung to her father's every word. She knew instinctively and by listening to heated, passionate discussions between her father and grandfather that she would never accept what life offered without questioning everything around her. When everyone else was satisfied with a situation, her father would undoubtedly push the envelope and try to change things. This got him into trouble growing up but it also helped him become a successful technology executive. In stark contrast, Wooldridge's mother, Stephanie, would say, "this is the way the religion says it is and they are right, so believe it."

Wooldridge recalls a time in her childhood when her father was faced with a stressful work situation that smacked of racism in which he lost a major business deal. Her father broke down and cried in the car with her mother. To her recollection, this was the only time her dad ever cried, at least when she was present. These rare moments when her dad showed vulnerability had a powerful influence on Wooldridge too. "Regardless of the racism, hardships he endured, and the anger he sometimes couldn't find a way to express constructively," Juana says, "he was able to face everything and overcome it. In my eyes, my father is a hero." To see her father rise above challenges helped Wooldridge do the same. She gained a lot of her father's spirit and leadership qualities. Always a leader, never a follower, Wooldridge didn't realize until later in life that these skills would come in handy. Nor did she know she would be faced with painful decisions that would forever change the course of her life.

Her father found a way to harness his dynamism and make it work for him. He has always been results-driven and he skillfully mastered the art of self-discipline. For years he would run five miles or more every single day but eventually had to cut down on the mileage because of a knee injury he sustained playing college football that began to bother him as he got older. According to Wooldridge, her father possesses a fierce determination and fears nothing. "He never let anything bring him down, never let any doors shut and he wasn't about to let his circumstances keep him where he was," says Juana.

Wooldridge considers her father a man of many talents and layers. He is extremely outspoken and a master debater, always up for a good, constructive argument about politics, world events, or issues affecting the community. He is also a gentle, loving soul. David has a quick wit and is considered a bit of a comedian in the family. He loves to say things, especially at family gatherings, that shock everyone, leaving family members laughing hysterically in wide-eyed disbelief. Most important, Wooldridge feels that her father has a heart of gold. When Juana's brother, Malcolm, became a successful football player in grade school and later in high school, David made sure his son and some of his teammates, particularly those who didn't have fathers in the home, were encouraged and given positive reinforcement. He took the time to get to know Malcolm's teammates and made it a priority to take them all out to eat regularly. He would have the boys over to the Wooldridge home where he talked with and got to know them. He became a role model for the young men.

Wooldridge recalls that she was asked to give a speech for her eighth grade graduation, not because she was valedictorian, but because she was a good student known to speak out passionately on issues. Her father listened intently as she delivered her speech. After the graduation, he expressed how very proud he was of her. In typical David fashion, he explained exactly why he was proud, telling her that she spoke so well and so clearly. This was a memorable moment for Wooldridge because making her dad proud was important to her. What she longed for most was quality time with her father. What she lacked in quality time with her dad in her early years, she gained as she got older, primarily watching gangster movies and football, learning the nuances of sports from him and having in depth discussions about life. They became even closer when she became an adult. Wooldridge feels that earlier in his life, her father had a difficult time identifying with or relating to women—and Wooldridge has become a strong woman. She worked hard to find the common ground between them. Today, Wooldridge co-hosts a sports talk radio show and feels comfortable talking sports with her male counterparts due in large part to her relationship with her father. Much of her sports knowledge and her love for football come from the quality time she spent with her dad watching and talking about sports.

Soon after Wooldridge's parents married in 1974, her mother, Stephanie, became a devout Jehovah Witness. As Wooldridge explains, "When the Jehovah's Witnesses came to my mother's door, my father was an alcoholic and a drug addict. They gave her a lot of peace and she clung to that organization." Wooldridge learned from her mother to accept that the Jehovah's Witness teachings and lifestyle were right and true. She embraced the religion faithfully as a young girl, taking on the role of a de facto parent to her brother and sisters to help her mother and make sure all of the Wooldridge children were ready to go to the weekly meetings on time.

Whenever she came home from church she would say to her father, "Daddy, I believe this is the way it is, this is the way God is."

David would reply, "How can this be?"

Wooldridge would plop down on the couch next to her dad, Bible in hand, and debate her father about the teachings of the Jehovah's Witnesses. He would ask her a question and she would answer him, citing the particular bible verse that related to their discussion. Her dad would demand that she explain her interpretation based on her growing knowledge of religion and spirituality. He treated her like an adult when they debated religious beliefs and raised questions that most people wouldn't even think to ask. "You believe this? Well, explain it to me," David would demand of his daughter. She had to know why she believed what she believed. These were valuable lessons for Wooldridge because they taught her how to debate like her father and made her very good at explaining her beliefs and supporting her arguments. She wasn't afraid to debate anyone. Growing up there were times Wooldridge would visit friends and instead of playing with dolls or doing what most young girls do, she would sit at the kitchen table with her friends' parents and talk religion or politics.

As she grew older, something about the Jehovah's Witness religion just didn't feel right in her spirit. Once the questions began to spill from her lips, she realized she was heading down a path of no return. She had been loved and respected within the organization for much of her young life. It is understandable then that Wooldridge's decision to leave was a huge disappointment to her mother and the entire organization. Soon she found herself completely ostracized from the religion and from her mother and sisters. "As a Jehovah's Witness, it's all your life, all your friends.

I was taught it every single day," says Juana. "I knew the consequences of leaving. I knew leaving the religion was leaving my family." Wooldridge was faced with the most difficult choice any young woman would have to make. Do you give up your family or do you give up your sense of self to accept religious teachings that are at best unsettling, and at worst, completely wrong in your eyes? Wooldridge found herself in an untenable position. She understood at her very core that walking away was a losing proposition with her mother and sisters, and for a while she wasn't sure she could withstand the ostracism sparked by her decision.

During this time, Wooldridge had to ask questions about what she really believed about God and to trust the healing process in order to reconnect with God. She believes very much in God's love and has learned from her own pain not to ostracize or judge people. Still today, Wooldridge believes that her upbringing was perfect for her and in studying Jesus. She learned that He spoke about love, and He didn't always do what everybody thought He should do. "In my studies of the bible I understood that Jesus was very much into saying that rules were made to protect and help the people," says Juana. "When something wasn't right, Jesus would stand up against everyone and do the right thing. That became my new source of religion, and I developed a very personal relationship with God that helped me develop my own type of ministry."

David made sure that his daughter, now officially estranged from her mother and sisters—three of the people who meant the world to her—was taken care of along with his grandson, Blace.

He made sure they could leave the religion. He also provided financial support and a shoulder to cry on when she needed one. Her dad became her rock during this difficult time. Essentially, David helped his daughter find her freedom and her voice. The consequence, of course, is that her mother and sisters were no longer allowed to talk to her or help her in any way. "My family has been completely severed, and it's been very hard on my dad too because the religion really didn't leave room for my dad to *not* be a Witness," says Juana.

Upon leaving the religion, Wooldridge went into a severe depression, sleeping for days at a time. She simply could not pull herself out of bed. She couldn't pray to God for years and carried the terrible feeling that God was unhappy with her. It took a long time, and she felt deeply isolated. Wooldridge eventually found the strength to put one foot in front of the other and move forward with her life. She learned to smile again. She learned to laugh again. She learned to forgive herself and others. She had the enduring support of her father and her father's side of the family. Her paternal grandparents, aunts, uncles and many cousins made sure she knew that in them, she would always, always have family. They stepped in and were there for her. The family made sure she and Blace were at every holiday gathering and family outing. This extraordinary family wrapped their arms around her during her difficult journey. Their support was tremendous and with her father next to her every step of the way, she gained the courage to stand up again, and to take a stand. "I had no idea that I had been born to do it, but I was being setup to stand up for what I believe in," Juana says. "It took a good ten years of my life, but I took a stand." Currently Wooldridge studies ministry leadership through Ohio Christian University's online curriculum and eventually plans to go to seminary.

Wooldridge currently has no personal relationship with her mother, Stephanie. Theirs is considered a business relationship. She can no longer go to her mother's house for dinner, ask her for a ride in her car, or rely on her mother if there was ever an emergency. Wooldridge has come to accept this reality. In spite of the broken family ties, Stephanie babysits her grandson, Blace, during the week while Wooldridge works and studies. Wooldridge pays her mother to care for her child and feels to this day that she is a wonderful mother and grandmother. Wooldridge knows that her mother loves Blace unconditionally. She understands too that her mother teaches Blace about the Jehovah's Witness religion. She readily admits that it comes with the territory, but she talks with Blace each day, never undermining her mother, but instead making sure that she ever so carefully teaches her son about a worldly approach to life and God— the kind of approach that she believes in and embraces.

Looking beneath the surface of this broken mother-daughter relationship, it is easy to see that Blace has essentially become the tie that binds, weaving their lives together. Wooldridge and Stephanie may never again share a warm embrace. Wooldridge may never again receive the thoughtful advice her mother gave throughout her childhood. However, through Blace, a handsome, energetic, and very smart little boy, they share unspoken love that may never be verbalized or understood by others. They love and need each other in ways that religious differences can never tear apart.

Wooldridge doesn't blame her mother or her father for any of the hardships the Wooldridge family endured, and she will always hold a special place in her heart for her mother. "My mom did the best she could," says Juana. "She believes in her religion, and that's her life, so I accept that and I'm not mad at her at all. I love my family and I know they think that what they are doing is the right thing to do. They believe they are in the true religion and that they should cut off members that leave their organization. I don't want them to hurt their conscience toward God."

Despite hardships, Wooldridge is comforted knowing that her father is still by her side, supporting her in good times and in bad. In her eyes, her dad has always been a shining example of a wonderful African American father. "My dad has always taken care of his family, and when I was in a very difficult place, my father never abandoned me," says Juana. "No matter what anybody says or does, he has always been there to help me get on my feet and get my own life together. My father is very giving. He is such a huge part of Blace's life too. He's always there." Ultimately, Wooldridge is happy with her decisions and her life—a life her father helped shape and define.

John Rogers, Jr.

Chief Investment Officer

"My father's love showed up in a million ways."

Treating others fairly, being a man of his word, upholding family values and lest we forget, love for the game of basketball—these core values and personal passions have fueled John W. Rogers, Jr. his entire life, inspired by life lessons from his father, the Honorable John W. Rogers, Sr.

In 1983, Rogers founded Ariel Investments to focus on undervalued small and medium-sized companies. Today, he is regularly featured and quoted in a wide variety of broadcast and print publications and is a contributing columnist to *Forbes*. Beyond Ariel, Rogers serves as a board member of Exelon Corporation and McDonald's Corporation. He is a trustee of the University of Chicago, where he also chairs the board of the University of Chicago Laboratory School and a director of the Robert F. Kennedy Center for Justice and Human Rights. In 2008, he was awarded his alma mater, Princeton University's highest honor, the Woodrow Wilson Award, presented each year to the alumnus whose career embodies a commitment to national service. Following the 2008 election of his long-time friend President Barack Obama, Rogers served as co-chair for the Presidential Inaugural Committee.

The Honorable John W. Rogers, Sr. was born in Knoxville, Tennessee in 1918 and came of age in the height of the Great Depression. He had a very difficult upbringing, losing both his mother and father by the time he was twelve years old. He also lost several sisters to tuberculosis. His one surviving sister, Geraldine, with whom he was very close, moved with him from their hometown of Knoxville to Chicago to live with an uncle who agreed to take them in. While the uncle was kind-hearted, John, Sr. and Geraldine were not *his* children, and he was not the nurturing type. One can imagine how difficult it was for a man to take in two orphaned children who had no resources and nowhere else to go. Judge Rogers soon realized that he had to make it on his own and decided that education would be his path to success.

He was exceptional in math and an all-around good student at Tilden Technical High School on Chicago's South Side. After graduating from high school Judge Rogers enrolled in Chicago Teachers College, which later became Chicago State University. He worked his way through college as a short-order cook and held several odd jobs to pay for school. John, Sr., who spent his childhood enamored with airplanes and dreaming of flight, became a licensed pilot and enlisted in the Air Force. He served in the legendary 99th Pursuit Squadron of the Tuskegee Airmen—the first African American pilots in the U.S. military. Judge Rogers excelled as a combat pilot, rising to the rank of captain and flying on more than 100 missions in the war. "He was extremely proud of being part of that pioneering first group of fighter pilots that went overseas," says John. "He was quite proud of the fact that he had supported his country in a time of need."

Judge Rogers has always been determined, driven, and purposeful. When he returned to Chicago after World War II in 1945, he decided to go to law school. He discovered that war vets could pursue college and advanced degrees through the GI Bill. The GI Bill created a comprehensive package of benefits, including financial assistance for higher education, for veterans of U.S. military service. The benefits of the GI Bill were intended to help veterans readjust to civilian life following service to their country. Approximately 7.8 million World War II veterans received benefits under the original GI Bill, and 2.2 million of those used the program for higher education. By 1947 half of all college students were veterans. Judge Rogers felt that if the government would pay for him to earn an advanced degree, he should go to a top law school. He also knew that a University of Chicago law degree would carry a lot of weight, and surely it would pave the way for a secure financial future.

When the elder Rogers first applied to the University of Chicago Law School, the school administrator's did not want to accept him. He returned dressed neatly and confidently in his captain's uniform and essentially argued his way into school. He met Chicago born and bred, Jewel Stradford, in the first couple of days after he arrived on campus. Jewel was also a law student who would later blaze trails and set the bar extraordinarily high for women, particularly African American women. In 1946, she became the first African American woman to graduate from the University of Chicago Law School. Judge Rogers and Jewel married in 1946 and together they started a law firm in 1949. Both became prominent attorneys, and in 1963, Jewel became the first African American woman to argue a case before the United States Supreme Court. She held high posts in the Nixon and Bush Administrations and became the first female deputy solicitor general of the United States, an official in the administration of President George H. W. Bush.

As he practiced law, the elder Rogers began to realize that a culture of segregation and discrimination was inherent in the system. He decided that the way to have the financially secure future he dreamt of along with a pension was to go into politics and work with the Democratic machine with the goal of becoming a judge. Overcoming the era's racial barriers, Judge Rogers was ultimately appointed a Cook County Juvenile Court judge, serving on the bench for 21 years. According to John Jr., "Being a lawyer taught my dad how to think. He also loved being a juvenile court judge because he could play parent to all of these kids who had troubled lives, kind of like he had. He loved his work, but at the same time I do think his passion for financial security drove him as well."

Though Judge Rogers has always been considered quiet and never the life of the party, he has been characterized as a brutally honest man because he believed in telling the truth. He has also been portrayed as terribly direct sometimes, saying things that might be deemed by some as borderline inappropriate. Nonetheless, people have always respected him because he has never put on any airs, and has remained humble. There is never a question of his honesty or integrity and he has always been nice and cordial to everyone he meets. Still, he held formidable opinions and had quite a temper in the height of his career. Seeing him angry was never high on anyone's list, especially staff, colleagues, and his son.

John, Sr. and Jewel were married nearly twelve years when, in 1958, they welcomed their only child, John, Jr. into the world. As he grew up, his parents set examples of excellence that have guided him throughout his life. Moreover, they established high expectations that he would grow up to be a man of character and integrity no matter which professional path he chose. Judge Rogers led his son on the road to financial security, buying him stocks that paid dividends every Christmas when he was a kid and every birthday after he turned twelve years old. Though his parents divorced in 1961, Rogers spent every weekend with his father who came to get him on Saturday afternoons and dropped him off at school on Monday mornings.

Judge Rogers was a strict but fair disciplinarian who set very clear rules for his son. By a certain age, it was expected that Rogers would have a checking account. At age twelve he had to have a stock market account. At age sixteen, his father insisted that he have a summer job. Rogers recalls having a savings account but with that savings account came pedantic guidelines and expectations that were non-negotiable.

Integrity was also a major lesson that Judge Rogers worked hard to teach his only son. Over and over again, he made it clear that telling the truth was incredibly important and there was no excuse for dishonesty whatsoever. His father also made sure he learned that being late and not living up to commitments to other people were totally unacceptable. He taught Rogers that, "If you promised you were going to do something, you do it and you live up to your word." He was relentless about the things that were important to him and made sure his son upheld the Rogers' core values. If Judge Rogers lost his temper, it was brutal no matter the circumstances. For instance, if Rogers went to see a movie with his father and in the middle of the movie he said or did something his father felt wasn't right, the elder Rogers would quickly tell him to gather his belongings and they would get up and leave. There were no second chances, and John Sr.'s word was law. If Rogers was supposed to do something and he didn't do it, he would suffer the consequences, which sometimes included spankings.

Did Rogers ever feel that his dad's rules were relentless? Did he ever want to tell his dad to cut him some slack? Certainly. On the one hand, he understood, appreciated, and respected his father's values that seemed morally right. And because he had a healthy dose of respect for his father, he abided by the rules. On the other hand, there were times when he wished his father would indeed give him a break. Unfortunately, there were no breaks given in his father's house. Judge Rogers meant business. Rogers understood that he had to be home on time and he knew there were consequences for not doing the dishes or making his bed, and as a kid he couldn't help but think about the what ifs: *What if my dad bought me a toy for Christmas instead of a stock certificate? What if I got a chance to run and play outside more instead of washing the dishes?* As an adult, John is honest with himself about the affect his dad's lessons had on him. Under his father's rules he missed out on a *laissez-faire* type of childhood that some of his friends enjoyed, but he realizes he wouldn't be where he is today without them.

Rogers' mother stood at the opposite end of the parental spectrum, which, according to John was possibly more problematic than the strict rules that governed life with his father. Fortunately, the fact that their parenting styles were antithetical never caused conflict between John, Sr. and Jewel. If they did have moments of disagreement, they were smart enough not to disagree in front of their son or put him in the middle of conflict. Both attorneys were insistent that nothing they did would negatively impact their son's upbringing.

As he grew older, they joked about how some of his dad's rules were, "kind of crazy" including his need to be fiscally conservative to a fault. "My dad would keep track of every penny. We dined at Mr. Stephen's for dinner on Saturday nights. When he got the bill he insisted on adding up everything to make sure it really cost $11.73 and he was sure to get his change back," John reminisced with a laugh. Strict rules notwithstanding, every weekend father and son kept their regular routine. They went bowling followed by dinner at Mr. Stephen's restaurant in the Prairie Shores neighborhood of Chicago, and they had the same seats at the Chicago White Sox games on Sunday afternoons. Theirs was a very special routine, and like Judge Rogers' rules, their father and son quality time was non-negotiable.

Although Judge Rogers worked seven days a week including Christmas, Thanksgiving, and birthdays, one thing his son understood with certainty is that he was the center of his dad's universe. There was never a question in John's mind that he was his dad's priority. "It was all about me," he admits. "I know that can cause problems and selfishness in some kids, but it was great to know that I was loved and cared about. I was the focus."

The elder John's stockbroker, Stacy Adams, the first African American stockbroker on LaSalle Street in Chicago's famed financial district, became a role model for young Rogers while a student at Harvard St. George Elementary School and later, at the University of Chicago Laboratory High School. Rogers spent a lot of time after school in Stacy's office where he would watch the ticker tape go by. With Stacy's guidance and influence, John began to buy and sell stocks. Stacy, whose friendship proved invaluable to the budding investment broker, even inspired John to study economics at Princeton University, where he also became captain of the varsity basketball team during his senior year.

Anyone who knows Rogers understands that basketball is one of his great passions. In fact, he earned the honor of being the first person to beat Michael Jordan to three points in a one-on-one game during Jordan's fantasy camp—arguably the greatest sports moment of John's life. Well before reigning supreme over Jordan, Rogers offers that it was a lucky coincidence that he got to attend Princeton University *and* play basketball for the Ivy League institution. Most would contend that it had everything to do with his excellent grades in addition to the basketball skills he cultivated as a high school student-athlete.

Rogers' four years at Princeton gave him the chance to realize some of his loftiest athletic dreams. At the end of his junior year, he got his shot and started the last three games. In the game against Brown University, he scored 20 points leading Princeton to the win. Unbeknownst to him, the judge had flown out to New Jersey that Friday afternoon to surprise him at the game. Rogers didn't know his dad was there until he walked off the court with his head held high, letting the victory sink in. It was a very fortunate time in John's life, and he is grateful that he can look back and remember that his father was there to share the moment with him. They celebrated the victory in a *big* way—eating burgers and fries at McDonald's with one of Rogers' closest friends on the team.

His father sent him encouraging notes while he was in college congratulating him on many of his academic accomplishments. These notes meant a great deal to Rogers. He reflected on talks he had with his father in the context of how men relate or do not relate to their sons. Rogers recalls that his father told him enough times one way or another, directly or indirectly, how proud he was and how deeply he loved him. Not surprisingly, his father talked about him to everyone who would listen. "I never had to question how he felt about who I was becoming and that always made me feel good," says John.

After graduating with a degree in economics from Princeton University in 1980, he took a job with William Blair and Company, where he was the first African American professional to work at the then 400-employee company. After spending two and a half years at William Blair, Rogers came up with an innovative and effective investment strategy focusing on small and midcap undervalued stocks—a sort of Warren Buffett philosophy—in trying to find good small and midsize businesses that were out of favor selling at good, cheap prices.

Rogers discovered there had never been an African American mutual fund company or money management firm in the country's history. Before taking the entrepreneurial leap, he looked at the landscape of African American success stories including role models, John Johnson, founder of Johnson Publishing Company, and George Johnson, founder of Johnson Products Company. He made up his mind that he too could become a successful business owner. Like his father, self-doubt never entered his mind, and he felt at age twenty-four that he could create something really special in forming a new money management firm.

Ariel, now Ariel Investments, was started in 1983 on the basic principle of targeting undervalued companies that show great potential for growth. For John it's been both a love affair and a tremendous challenge. "Ariel is still the only minority-owned mutual fund company listed in the newspaper every morning in *USA Today*," John says. "It's still kind of remarkable that you've got thousands of mutual funds, and we are the one sole minority-owned fund family that has become established. We have become pioneers in the industry, and we're making history."

Rogers often hears his father's voice when he makes decisions that have long-term business implications, particularly when dealing with matters that involve honoring commitments. Many years ago Ariel had a partnership with Calvert Group that after several years was no longer working. With Rogers at the helm, Ariel developed a plan to sever ties and focus on building the Ariel Mutual Funds brand, no longer maintaining any affiliation with Calvert Group. Instead of trying to walk away or get into litigation over the split, Rogers and his partners made the decision to honor their commitment by negotiating a fair deal. "It was like a divorce, and we had to pay approximately $4 million to buy our freedom, but I knew it was the right thing to do," says John. "Knock on wood, nothing has ever happened in nearly thirty years in business from an ethical or moral standpoint that has been an issue from our perspective. We treat everyone fairly. It comes from the values my father taught me. From the very beginning we have had a board of directors and we have an outside audit firm audit our books every year. We try to run the company in a first-class way to make sure we never get into any regulatory or tax issues with the IRS, and that's my dad's voice. He always told me: 'Honor your commitments, pay your bills, and pay them on time.'"

As Rogers became a successful business owner, he was able to turn the tables and teach his father a few life lessons. He is much more of a risk taker, financially and in life, than his dad. He taught the judge that his business could have been larger and his career could have been more successful if he had been willing to take more risks including his approach to hiring staff, building the office out and doing things to build on the future. Rogers became an example of an outspoken businessman, not because this was his inherent personality, but because he understood the importance of giving of his time, talent and treasures in the interest of helping others. Rogers feels that a critical part of his success as a businessman and entrepreneur stems from exposure—being out there in front of people, giving speeches, showing up at fundraisers, spending time at community organizations, and volunteering to help others. Ultimately this sense of selflessness and honoring his commitment to others has created goodwill while helping him accomplish some of the things he wanted to accomplish in the community.

One of the many reasons Rogers has enjoyed such success, particularly as a member of Chicago's civic community where he serves on numerous boards, is because people know they can count on him. Being true to his word and fulfilling commitments are overarching principles that show up in dozens of decisions John has made. Conversely, Judge Rogers went to the office seven days a week, came home, and worked some more. He didn't go anywhere until he got involved in democratic politics prompting him to attend second ward meetings and precinct captain meetings.

Judge Rogers wasn't willing to do the relationship building that John found so important. Later in his career as a judge, he began to see through his son's eyes and experiences that just maybe he'd been too inwardly focused, not wanting to go to that extra cocktail party or get involved in more board work and philanthropic endeavors. Perhaps it would have been helpful, but maybe the most important lesson for Judge Rogers stems from the idea that his son taught him a few things that he hadn't considered—proof that there is intrinsic value in learning from your own kids no matter how successful one becomes.

So many of the decisions Rogers has made throughout his life are centered on living up to commitments and in some ways, his father's expectations. Rogers spent most of his young life observing and being molded into a financially astute, self-assured man. It stands to reason then that he would want to honor his father by living an exemplary, respectful, and respectable life filled with integrity and sound moral judgment. He has passed many of these values on to his only child, Victoria, who like her father, attended the University of Chicago Laboratory Schools but instead of following in her dad's footsteps and attending Princeton, she, according to Rogers, "went with the enemy camp" and earned a Bachelor's degree in art history from Yale University. In raising Victoria, Rogers tried to blend the best of both of his father and his mother's parenting styles. John's former wife, Victoria's mother, Desiree Rogers, chief executive officer of Johnson Publishing Company, has always been a very supportive, wonderful mom.

In terms of instilling values, Rogers, with support from Desiree, tried to focus on the best and most important values from his father and then eliminate the other kinds of rules that didn't fit their lifestyle. He taught Victoria the importance of living up to her commitments—a lesson passed down from her grandfather. "When I brought Victoria up, if she said she made a commitment to do something and tried to wiggle out of it, that was unacceptable," says John. He also taught her to always look out for her friends, listen to them, and look for ways to help when needed. "Other than that, my rules for Victoria have been pretty simple."

As Victoria was growing up, the Rogers family sometimes vacationed with other families. During vacations Rogers observed other parents correcting behavior every few minutes— from what to eat to what not to eat, from when to stop running to when to sit still. Rogers never saw the need to have a heavy-handed approach in raising his daughter. He trusted Victoria and had faith in her ability to think for herself. "I got that from Lab School and from my mom," says John. "I wasn't going to try to micromanage her and create all kinds arbitrary rules." Rogers wanted his daughter to study and get good grades because she *wanted* to, not because there was some threat hanging over her head. Rogers felt that she would be more effective, more successful, and happier if he didn't create that environment of fear. "I didn't want her to be afraid to come home and show me her report card," says John. "That was a different approach then my dad had."

Today at age ninety-four, the Honorable John W. Rogers, Sr., enjoys a quiet life with his second wife, Gwen Laroche Rogers, PhD. Together they live in a lovely condominium overlooking Lake Michigan in the beautiful Hyde Park neighborhood of Chicago.

Rogers is forever grateful for the lessons he learned from the man who epitomizes fairness, honor, and integrity. He is filled with pride when he talks about all that his father has accomplished as a father, grandfather, husband, Tuskegee Airman, attorney, and judge. In Rogers' eyes, his father "has always been a man of his word. His sense of fairness is critical. His sense of honesty is critical, and I appreciate that my father's love showed up in a million ways."

Dr. Velma Scantlebury, MD

Transplant Surgeon

"My father demonstrates to us that it's all about family, it's all about love and it's all about helping others."

Dr. Velma Patricia Scantlebury is a gift. A gift to the field of medicine, a gift to her family, a gift to those blessed with a new kidney by the miracle of her steady hands and brilliant mind. She is also a gift to those who have the opportunity to hear the smile in her voice as she warmly describes the strength and love she receives from her father, Delacey Scantlebury, who recently celebrated his ninety-first birthday.

Scantlebury is the first African American female kidney transplant surgeon and associate director of the Kidney Transplant Program at Christiana Care Health Systems in Delaware. Born October 6, 1955 in St. Michael, Barbados, she is the youngest of seven children. She comes from humble beginnings on the island of Barbados from which generations of her family hail. This distinguished and celebrated physician received her early education at the Alleyne School in St. Andrew, Barbados until she came to the United States with her father and three of her six siblings. Prior, her oldest sister traveled to England to continue her studies and passed away from an illness when Scantlebury was eight years old. Her mother, Kathleen, journeyed to the US a few years before the rest of the family to find work and help pave the way for an American education for her children, which she and her husband agreed would be beneficial for Scantlebury, who at the time began to express an interest in medicine. As a student at the Alleyne School, Scantlebury had the simple assignment of writing an essay entitled *My Career*. She thought about some of the career attributes that might interest her. Being her own boss, helping people and having a good deal of autonomy were high on her list. In addition, she wanted to learn more about the illness that took her older sister's life. She researched several career paths and decided to write about being a doctor. The more she researched the field of medicine, the more it spoke to her.

Scantlebury's early education in her native Barbados is in some ways reminiscent of the late Shirley Chisholm, the first African American woman elected to Congress and the first woman to run for the Democratic presidential nomination. Though Chisholm was born in the United States to immigrant parents, at the age of three she was sent to live with her strict grandmother in Barbados for seven years. In her 1970 autobiography, *Unbought and Unbossed,* Chisholm, an awe-inspiring, fearless politician and educator, described her Barbadian education: "Years later I would know what an important gift my parents had given me by seeing to it that I had my early education in the strict, traditional, British-style schools of Barbados. If I speak and write easily now, that early education is the main reason." Like Chisholm, Scantlebury benefited from a solid Barbadian education before coming to the US. It was on this Caribbean island in the West Indies under the watchful eye of her parents that she received the foundation and the discipline to follow her path to medical greatness.

When the family moved to the US, Scantlebury attended Prospect Heights High School in Brooklyn, New York. She has described the initial experience of attending the Brooklyn high school as terrifying. But the educational foundation from the Alleyne School gave her an edge and was the overriding factor that saw her through when she experienced a lack of encouragement in high school. When teachers questioned her ability to go on to college, her parents stepped in and convinced her that she should. She attended Long Island University, Brooklyn Campus on a four-year academic scholarship and graduated with an honors degree in biology. She went on to attend the esteemed College of Physicians and Surgeons at Columbia University School of Medicine.

Being a kidney transplant surgeon wasn't necessarily one of the specialties that piqued her interest when she entered medical school; it was pediatrics. Pediatrics was the first specialty she observed from going to her own pediatrician and asking lots of questions as a child in Barbados. This early exposure planted the seed, but when she got to Columbia Medical School and enrolled in her first gross anatomy class, her focus shifted and she was immediately interested in the whole idea of the body—dissecting, learning to cut into body parts, fixing and removing things. "That was it for me," says Velma. "I just knew I had to get my hands in there and be a surgeon." Thankfully, her father has been there to support her and express his profound pride with every new opportunity she has received as a transplant surgeon and every award she has won for outstanding advances in the medical field. She holds the National Kidney Foundation's Gift of Life Award, the Lifetime Achievement Award of the American Society of Minority Health and Transplant Professionals, as well as honorary Doctor of Science degrees from Seton Hill College and her alma mater Long Island University.

Scantlebury's parents, Delacey and Kathleen Scantlebury were both born in Belleplaine in the small parish of St. Andrew, Barbados. They met as teenagers, married in 1942, and had four boys and three girls. Scantlebury is the youngest of their seven children. Delacey was one of seven brothers raised by a single mother. His father moved to the United States when he was a young boy, so he has no real recollection of his father. Delacey's mother passed away when he just was fourteen. Scantlebury recalls her father once sharing the heartbreaking story of the day his mother, a stocky woman standing over six feet tall, died in her sleep. "She came home not feeling well after a long day at work. She went to bed early. My father heard her make a loud noise and a deep sigh in the middle of the night. She never woke up."

Upon the death of their mother, all seven of the Scantlebury boys were forced to grow up quickly. The older boys worked and went to school, and all of the boys managed to stay together, taking on household responsibilities for as long as they could. Eventually Delacey went to live with an aunt for a while and the brothers had no choice but to disperse, living with relatives or going off to find work and start lives of their own.

His mother's death taught him an important lesson about taking responsibility for his own life if he was going to make it in this world. He passed this lesson on to his own children: "If you want to do something, if you want to get out of a situation, if you want to better yourself, then you have to take on that responsibility. You can't necessarily depend on other people to get you where you want to go." This lesson was particularly apropos in young Delacey's life at a time when he was hoping to be hired for a particular job. Unfortunately, the supervisor in charge had other plans and took away his chance to get the position. The sense of rejection disappointed Delacey and made him angry, but it also made him to look beyond the position to ask himself, "What else can I do?"

Standing at this professional crossroads helped him make the decision to leave that part of the island in search of better opportunities. This was a pivotal time in his life, and if the supervisor hadn't unknowingly forced Delacey to move on, he would not have pushed himself to work harder for something greater. At twenty-three with his wife and children in tow, he moved to the city and was selected to go to the police academy for law enforcement training. Delacey went on to become a police officer in Barbados. As he told Scantlebury and all of his children, "It is difficult to take that leap when one door closes, but you just can't sit down and mope about what didn't happen to you. You have to pull yourself up and ask yourself how you can make something out of this experience." Scantlebury is proud that her father always taught them that the opportunity you thought was going to come your way may not come, but every time one door closes, another opens up and you have to see the positive side of even the most negative experiences.

Scantlebury shares that her father's dreams have been fulfilled through his children. He takes great pride in seeing them accomplish things he wasn't able to accomplish. Each time he saw his sons and daughters advance to another grade, learn a new skill, discover something fanciful about the world, or profess their love for math, science, business or the arts, he felt a sense of pride. His dream was to see each of his children grow up, go to college, and become successful professionals no matter where their talents took them. Scantlebury intimates that her father is the type of person who has always reached out to help others regardless of how little he had. He unfailingly made sure his children and those he loved were taken care of. For a young man with seven kids that was a lot of responsibility, but he did what he had to do. Scantlebury recalls a time when sending his children to school became a hardship, especially when he and the kids were still in Barbados and his wife had already gone to New York. Having to financially and emotionally support each and every one of the children was tough, but he made sure they each received a good education, a solid foundation, and lots of love. "We didn't have a whole lot, but with my dad being a policeman the opportunities the police force offered sort of made up for the things that at times he wasn't able to give us," Velma shares. "The only party we received was when we went to the police officers' family Christmas party and we each got one toy. Our family otherwise couldn't afford these things."

Living with limited means meant having to defer many of the material things she and her siblings might have wanted. Despite the lean times, the Scantlebury family has always been a happy, tight-knit family. The brilliant surgeon recalls that although they didn't have a television growing up, her father and brothers, who are all very funny, spent time telling jokes and stories that made everyone laugh so hard until it hurt. To this very day when the family gets together, they spend time laughing and talking so much that her husband refers to her family as a loud, garrulous bunch. Scantlebury grew up wondering, "Doesn't everyone do this?" thinking that the best things in life were being close to one's family and telling jokes. For her family, this was the norm—and a beautiful norm at that.

When the family moved to New York, Delacey worked in security at Merrill Lynch until he retired. Fortunately for the family, he worked the early shift from 7am to 3pm which allowed him to be home by the time his children walked through the door, books in tow, after a busy school day. Generally Kathleen worked a later shift, first as a housekeeper and later as a nurse's aide. Delacey spent time talking and laughing with his children and taking them to afternoon activities. Kathleen made the family meals in the early days, but eventually he cooked for the family and became the family chef in later years. According to Scantlebury, her dear father still loves to cook and bake. "As old as my brothers are and as old as my dad is, I always ask my brothers, 'Why are you going to dad's house for food? You should be feeding him!'" laughs Velma.

Today, Scantlebury's sister does most of the cooking but on Saturdays when Delacey knows his family is coming by to spend the day, he still makes cou-cou, the national dish of Barbados. Cou-cou, a traditional African dish made of corn meal and okra, requires the chef to have a great deal of muscle strength because it must be churned over and over with a big wooden paddle until it is a smooth texture and the right consistency. Delacey still has the strength and the desire to make cou-cou for his family. He enjoys sitting around the table, eating and laughing with wife, children, and grandkids, very much like the family did in years past.

Outside of schoolwork, Delacey insisted that his children find something beneficial to do with their time—from cleaning someone's yard for a few pennies to providing help to neighbors or family members out of the kindness of their hearts. Delacey also embraced family time and rewarded the kids for being good students. What they lacked in material things they more than made up for when it was time to pack up the car and take family trips. Scantlebury remembers family trips as some of the best times of her life. Their time together meant everything to her and taught her that being rich didn't mean having lots of money or material things. It meant thanking God every day for the many blessings He bestowed and spending time enjoying family.

Scantlebury describes her father as an easygoing, loving, people person. Even today he is the kind of gentleman who makes regular trips to the local store and has a conversation with everyone he meets along the way. His children, especially those who still live close by, see him on the corner talking to neighbors and members of his Brooklyn community. "How ya' doin'?" or "What's up today?" Delacey will ask a neighbor walking by. In addition to being affable, he looks out for just about everybody, whether it's the young family across the street or fellow seniors. "Even when my father was in his seventies and eighties he would say, 'I have to go pick up the older folks to make sure they get to church,'" recalls an incredulous Velma. "You're in that category too!" was often her witty reply to her father. Through the years, Scantlebury's mother has lovingly complained about how her husband was always busy helping others. This annoyed her because she had a list of things for him to do at home. She knows, however, that her husband has a big heart, always looking out for others. Even though he had mouths to feed, he never hesitated to open his home to someone in need of a meal or a place to stay.

No matter how easygoing Delacey has been all his life, when he got upset with young Velma or his other children, they got an earful and sometimes more. Their father was strict and she can recall the whippings he handed out especially to her brothers. The boys insist, however, that by the time Scantlebury was growing up, their dad was tired. Thus, she didn't get much of the harsh treatment they remember receiving. As a father, he was very opinionated when it came to what he liked and didn't like. Scantlebury admits that her dad was hard on all of the kids, and in retrospect he could have done some things differently. Nevertheless, she understands and respects him for being present and taking the time to raise them in the way that he saw fit. She recalls with laughter times when the Scantlebury kids were dumbfounded that their all-knowing parents found out about the kid's wrongdoings before they even made it home from school. "There must have been little birdies that flew all the way home before we got there so my dad and mom knew what happened before we hit the front steps!" Velma admits that she probably got into less trouble than her brothers because she was the reader of the family who read as many books as possible. "It's hard to get into trouble when your head is in a book," Velma reflects.

Like most kids, Scantlebury often agonized over what her parents would think or how they feel about the grades she brought home or decisions she made. She felt genuine trepidation over telling them certain things because she was so scared of what their reaction would be. One might argue that this was wasted energy for an overachieving young girl who was perhaps too hard on herself. "I would build up all this energy and find the courage to come out and say what it is I wanted to say," says Velma. "And my father and mother would look at me and say, 'Is that it? That doesn't bother us. You are our child and whatever you do we will stand behind you.'" Her parents reaffirmed that as long as she had given it her all–no matter the outcome–they supported her 110 percent. This type of support in the Scantlebury household equated to true, unconditional love and made Scantlebury feel that she could accomplish anything. To this day, her dad still tells her how absolutely proud he is of what she has made of her life. "To me that's not my whole purpose in being the first African American female kidney transplant surgeon, but it does make me feel great about my decision to become a surgeon. My profession is something I felt I would be good at, and I always wanted to make a difference in the lives of other people," says Velma. "The fact that I've made my father so proud of me is icing on the cake."

Married for seventy years, together Delacey and Kathleen have built a life filled with love. Both have been blessed with relative good health and irrefutable longevity. They have fulfilled unspoken promises of providing their children with boundless opportunities and have set copious examples of how to make love last through life's ups and downs. They have taught their children the importance of listening and giving. Delacey embodies the true art of compromise and points out that in all relationships give and take are essential and that there must be a happy medium both partners can agree on. "My dad believes that if it means relinquishing the authoritative aspect of your personality in order to achieve harmony, then that's what you must do in order to maintain a healthy relationship with your partner," says Velma. She has observed over the years that her father is quick to concede in order to make peace. Even today when she visits him, he has a smile on his face and he sees the positive in everything. "Don't worry about it! Leave it to God!" Delacey is quick to share. "If you just trust the Lord, it will work out." Truer words have never been spoken. Today Kathleen, age eighty-six, suffers from dementia. Though her memory comes and goes, their love for one another, endures. She still calls her husband Lacey, the nickname she has had for him since they met in St. Andrews as teenagers. He's the only person she will allow to take care of her.

Delacey has been a leader and an elder in his non-denominational Christian church for at least two decades. The family is part of the same religion they believed in and followed in Barbados, and they have small gatherings in their home on Sunday mornings. He and Kathleen raised their children to understand that nothing is possible without having God in your life. They stressed the importance of giving the Almighty thanks and praise for everything they are able to accomplish. My father always said, "Everything you do is because of His goodness towards us and that there is a greater force out there beyond our ability to comprehend. None of this is of our own doing."

Scantlebury's dad taught her to always pray when confronted with a situation that she couldn't handle and God would provide an answer. This is one of her father's lessons that she still carries in her heart. For years she was professor of surgery and director of the University of South Alabama's Gulf Coast Regional Transplant Center where she trusted her instincts as a surgeon and felt overall that she made the right decisions in the best interest of her patients. Whenever she felt uncertain about a decision she would pick up the phone and call her father to ask him what he would do. "You know, I feel really unsure about this," she would share with her father. He would reply, "You did the best you could and that's all that you could do. That's all God asks of you. Do the best that you can and leave the rest to Him because it's out of your hands. The outcome is not yours to be determined." Her father has always given her sound advice and taught her to trust her faith in God.

For twenty-three years Scantlebury has been married to her longtime love, Harvey White, PhD. They have two lovely daughters, Aisha and Akela. Scantlebury and her husband have a different approach to parenting than that of her parents. They tend to give their girls more freedom and their lifestyle is different but they have taught Aisha and Akela some of the same values she learned as a child including the importance of education, having a sense of responsibility and understanding that what they do affects other people. Her expectations of her two daughters are very much the same as her father's expectations of his children. "We want them to have respect for themselves and have God in their lives," says Velma. "We tell them to give God thanks for everything and understand that the blessings bestowed upon them should never be taken for granted."

First African American female kidney transplant surgeon or not, Scantlebury is still "Daddy's Girl." He couldn't be prouder of her and never ceases to tell her so. When she is going through a difficult time, he calls one of his sons and asks them to look out for their sister. She and her dad have a great relationship, and if she hasn't seen him in awhile he doesn't hesitate to ask when she is coming to visit. They talk on a regular basis, and she tries to visit at least a couple times a month. Her sister and one of her brothers still live in Brooklyn, and when the Scantlebury clan comes home it's like a mini-family reunion. They eat and sit around the dining room table looking at old pictures, telling stories, reminiscing—and laughing until it hurts.

Without question, Scantlebury's father is one of the greatest people she has ever come to know. His love for life and his trust in God have given him such a warm spirit. It doesn't matter how much adversity or hardship he has experienced, he always has a positive attitude. "I think he is so at peace with his life that whenever his time is up, I'll know that he was content with all that he's done and all that he's seen his children accomplish," says Velma. "I know he has no regrets and he loves us all dearly because he demonstrates to us that it's all about family, it's all about love and it's all about helping others."

"What They See Is What They Will Be"

Motto of the 100 Black Men of America, Inc.

As the recent past President of the Detroit Chapter of the 100 Black Men of America, Inc., I saw firsthand the power and transformative impact of our motto, "What They See Is What They Will Be," on the youth we serve. This motto guides and influences our daily lives to serve as positive role models and to be constructive resources within our community. Leading and participating in this group of concerned and committed African American men who reach back to the youth in our community in order to help them envision and lead productive lives continues to be very rewarding and humbling.

While the first chapter of "The 100" began in New York City in 1963, a chapter did not exist in the Detroit area in the early 1960's as I was growing up. But, I witnessed firsthand every day a group of extraordinary African American men, including my own father, who embodied similar values and beliefs. They modeled for me and others what fathers were supposed to do; to care for, to nurture, to encourage, to guide, to develop, to discipline, to celebrate and most important, love their sons and daughters unconditionally. I was being mentored by this village of African American men, and I didn't even know it. I really didn't appreciate the significance of it until I was much older, but make no mistake, I now know what I saw being demonstrated by these men. They were "doing the right thing, the right way at the right time."

For example, I witnessed men like Andrew McLemore Sr., O'Neill Swanson Sr., and my own father Arthur Middlebrooks Sr., display the courage and aptitude to become successful entrepreneurs. These men started and led successful businesses in construction management, mortuary services, and adult foster care, respectively. I observed Dr. Willard Holt Sr. become the first African American department chair of anesthesiology at one of Detroit's leading hospitals. I experienced an Olympic gold medalist, Edward Gordon Jr., share his love and passion for science and athletics with his students while also teaching them the importance of academic excellence. His lessons were forerunners to today's emphasis on the role of the high performing student athlete.

Similarly, my passion for coaching and mentoring today comes from the outreach and patience that a then young family man by the name of Frederick Hudson showed me by way of his smooth style and dedication to his family. He spent countless hours "schooling" me and other young boys in the neighborhood about a range of life issues from girls and education to business and sports. I learned the art and importance of being a part of the "village watch" from Gilbert Fisher who always seemed to show up at the right time with the question, "Are you sure your parents would approve of this?" He and his wife Pat, my elementary school library teacher, always wanted to make sure I and the other kids on our block were focused on the right things. As I found myself running from neighborhood home to home, I saw very similar traits of quiet and studious strength in men like Drs. James Brown and Edgar Smith, Sr. who made their presence felt with their intellectual nature and calming approach through my regular interactions with them.

In addition to the challenges of providing for and raising their own sons and daughters, these men cared enough about me and the other children in our neighborhood to show us how to be men and engaged fathers. Through both their words and deeds they demonstrated to me how to stand strong by being respectful, present, and committed in the lives of their children and being men of high integrity and principles. Finally, while he did not know at the time, nor did I, that he would become my future father-in-law, James Rose Sr. took me into his home and offered me vivid examples of how to treat a wife with respect and as a full partner. He engaged me with his thoughtfulness and often encouraged my educational pursuits and business curiosity. His work ethic and dedication to family serves as a constant, vivid reminder for how I should approach each day.

I offer my sincere thanks, appreciation, and heartfelt respect to each of these men who helped to shape and guide me to become both the man and father I am today. I took many positive lessons about fatherhood from each of them and without consciously thinking about it, shared many of those same lessons with my own sons. I expect they too will pass along to future generations similar wisdom and many of the same positive life lessons from these extraordinary African American fathers from my Northwest Detroit neighborhood!

I offer my profound respect and appreciation to these great African American fathers and role models:

- Arthur "Chick" Middlebrooks Sr.

- James Rose Sr.

- Edward L. Gordon, Jr.

- Andrew G. McLemore, Sr.

- Frederick Hudson

- O'Neil D. Swanson, Sr.

- Dr. Willard S. Holt, Jr.

- Dr. James Brown

- Gilbert Fisher

- Dr. Edgar Smith, Sr.